Frank G. Ripel

Nagualism

Don Juan's secret teachings, the master of Carlos Castaneda

Orion

ISBN 978-1-4092-2612-3

Foreword

This book is the result of the secret knowledge I've been transmitted by a modern Mexican shaman and by an ancient sorcerer of Mexico, don Juan and the death opponent, knowledge that allowed me to follow the magical way of Nagualism.

All the topics I deal with in this book is the organic and systematic reconsideration of the subjects discussed by Carlos Castaneda, such as the perception's widening, the art of *stalking*, the practice of *dreaming* and the control of the *intent*.

With this work I did not confine myself to re-present the teachings already developed in Castaneda's books but, thanks to the teaching I have been given, I could bridge the gaps left by the well-known anthropologist. So I've been able to reveal all the gates of *dreaming*, all the abstract cores and all those knowledge concerning shamans' world, a separate reality.

Introduction

In the early 60s, Carlos Castaneda, a young anthropologist of California University, gets in touch with an old shaman, don Juan, a northern Mexico Yaqui Indio. Between the old shaman and the young anthropologist was born a new good friendship, an extraordinary mentor-disciple relationship that calls the "classic" one to the mind, such as that one between Socrates and Platone.

In those years Castaneda begins recording his training as an "apprentice sorcerer" and the partnership with his master will produce his books in which he describes his amazing apprenticeship.

Later, in the 70s, Carlos Castaneda is charged to have falsified data and reports contained in his books and to have provided a very different biography of himself, in contrast with document data and testimonies. But, in his second book – A Separate Reality – the well-known anthropologist reports, without making any mystery, what don Juan told him: "...a shaman's real name and the place where he lives must not be revealed". Therefore, there is nothing to be surprised if he falsified dates, places and names of his books' characters.

Then, in the 80s, Carlos Castaneda writes more and more accurate and detailed reports and other characters, besides don Juan and don Genaro, come on the scene, other Mexican modern shamans and an ancient sorcerer of Mexico, the death opponent.

Finally, in the 90s, Carlos Castaneda develops a system of

movements of the body that he calls Tensegrity and states: “To create those ‘movements’ I got inspiration from the magical passes found out by the sorcerers of ancient Mexico”.

On April 27th 1998 Carlos Castaneda dies, as a man, about ten o’clock in the morning and his body is cremated in Los Angeles. And it is undoubtedly interesting to notice what is written in his fifth book – The Second Ring of Power – in which la Gorda, a don Juan’s apprentice, reveals to Castaneda that ten o’clock a.m. would have been his new hour: “If you remain a man you will die around that time. If you become a sorcerer you will leave this world around that time”.

In Carlos Castaneda’s sixth book – The Eagle’s Gift – Silvio Manuel, a member of don Juan’s group, reveals to Castaneda that he was not the right Nagual – four-forked Nagual – to lead the group of apprentices. His bubble’s configuration had three compartments – three-forked Nagual – instead of four. There was another rule for him, that one of the three-forked Nagual.

As a Nagual, I decided to present this book in order that the secret teaching of Nagualism may be transmitted in its totality, as I received it – *silent knowledge* – by don Juan, my teacher, and by the death opponent, my benefactor. I can’t provide any evidence of my good faith, but this book provides the reader with the power to value the work I’ve done and to draw the proper conclusions.

The modern shamans, like in don Juan’s case, and the ancient sorcerers, like in the case of the death opponent, have three cycles. In the first and second cycle they are human beings, that is to say they have an organic body. The first cycle is when they are disciples, while in the second one they are teachers. Instead, in the third cycle they are no longer human, that is to say they haven’t a biological body anymore but they own an inorganic body. They come to give Nagualism’s secret teachings.

The teachers, in their second cycle, give the teaching to

their disciples on two levels.

The first level comprises the lessons for the right side, the state of normal perception that is the state of awareness needed to deal with every day life. In this condition – state of normal perception – the disciples receive the teachings that comprise basic concepts and procedures.

The second level, instead, comprises the lessons for the left side, the state of altered perception that is the state of awareness needed to receive the most significant part of the teachings. In this condition – state of intense perception – the disciples receive the teachings that comprise high concepts and particular procedures.

The advantage of the intense perception state lies in the fact that the mind is focused on any thing with extreme strength and perceptive clarity – tremendous concentration and acuteness of perception – out of the ordinary. Furthermore, the mind is able to grasp precisely the meaning of things with immediacy – acuteness of thought and increased comprehension – and the disciple's acting will be told by certain firmness. The disadvantage of this state lies in the fact that, when one comes back to the state of normal awareness, the mind is incapable of remembering what has happened. Only later, with a huge effort, the "task of remembering" can be carried out, the transformation from intense awareness to simple memory. Moreover, the disciple, when he is in the intense perception state, cannot be alone and must be looked after by the teacher who knows how to behave in that circumstance.

The teachers, during their third cycle, give the teaching to their disciples on a third level.

The third level comprises the lessons for the central part, state of silent perception that is the state of awareness needed to receive the most occult part of the teachings. In this state – state of silent perception – the disciples receive the teachings comprising concepts that derive from the silent knowledge – devoid of the annoying presence of spoken language – and procedures told directly by the *intent*, the *power* that rules universe's destiny.

Don Juan and the death opponent came to me, with their inorganic bodies, to give me Nagualism's secret teachings, essentially based on the knowledge of the Six Attentions (First, Second and Third Attention, Attention Zero, Fourth and Fifth Attention). Their knowledge and their power, directly related to *intent*'s silent knowledge, allowed me to write this book.

1

Secret knowledge

In all ancient traditions all over the world, the importance of plants with hallucinogenic properties lays in their power to produce, in human beings, altered perception states – not-ordinary reality – which allow gaining knowledge and power.

In don Juan's magical system four psychotropic plants are used: peyote (*Lophophora williamsii*), devil's grass (*Datura inoxia*) and two mushrooms: humito (*Psilocibe mexicana*) and muchomor (*Amanita muscaria*).

The use of peyote allows getting in touch with Mescalito, a magical being who teaches "the right way of living" and how to get the knowledge.

Peyote's buds are to be picked and swallowed, one at a time, chewing them slowly.

The use of the devil's grass, of humito and of muchomor allow the man to join his own "allied power", the personal ally.

Any species of *Datura* plant allows getting to the allied power, but a shaman must use only one species, that one which personally identifies itself with him.

The root of devil's grass must be prepared to make a potion that is of use to get the power, to experiment divination and for the magical flight. Whereas a potion made with the stem and the leaves is used to cure diseases and one made with the flowers is useful to hit enemies, driving them mad or making them die. Finally, a potion made with the seeds is of use to strengthen the shaman's *heart*.

Only one species of mushrooms – *Psilocibe mexicana* and *Amanita muscaria* – allow getting to the ally power and a shaman must be able to know them.

The humito (little smoke) is a smoke mixture made of dried mushrooms – *Psilocibe mexicana* – mixed with different parts of five other dried plants. The mixture is to be smoked in the magical pipe, which must be treated with loving care. The 'smoking' procedure consists of swallowing the mushroom's powder, which does not burn to ashes, and of inhaling the smoke of the other five plants. The mixture is used to experiment ecstasy, for the magical flight, for taking on animal form and for the *seeing*.

Muchomor is a mushroom – *Amanita muscaria* – which can be prepared in two ways. In the first one the mushroom is dried – preferably the cap only – and then rolled up into a ball. The 'eating' procedure consists of swallowing the mushroom, after a long chewing, in one instant. The *ball* is used to experiment ecstasy. In the second way the cap-covering red film is removed and dried. The 'smoking' procedure consists of inhaling the smoke thru the magical pipe. *Smoke* is of use to make the vision's power keener in *dreams*.

In don Juan's secret knowledge's context shamans teach how to use the peyote, the devil's grass and the humito when they are in their second cycle that is when they are human. Instead in their third cycle, when they are no longer human, they teach how to use the muchomor.

The muchomor – term used by Siberian shamans – is pre-eminently the "magical mushroom", whose connection with the man left marks in different areas of the world: Europe, Northern Asia, Northern and Southern Africa, Northern and Central America.

The shamanic use of *Amanita muscaria* left traces in Neolithic wall painting of far eastern Siberia, in Pre-Columbian

Maya codes of Yucatan and in the Rg-Veda, the most ancient religious document of India.

In the Rg-Veda more than one hundred verses are dedicated to this 'divine' plant from which an inebriating juice is obtained, the immortality drink, the Vedic Soma. And in the significant fresco of Plaincourant Abbey (XIII century), a locality in central France, we find it plainly represented between Adam and Eve to symbolize the knowledge tree's forbidden fruit, with the snake coiled around it.

The power contained in *Datura* plants and in some mushrooms, such as *Psilocibe mexicana* and *Amanita muscaria*, allows the shaman – man of knowledge – to get to the personal ally that must be tamed. And to tame it means, for the shaman, to intensify his own life, that is to make his own knowledge deeper and to take command of his own specific powers. Therefore, to have an ally means to have the knowledge and the power.

There are two ways of acting to get to one's ally. In the first way the learner takes the psychotropic substance for all the span of his apprenticeship and when he becomes a man of knowledge he meets his ally, which is the summa of all his knowledge and his power. In the second way, instead, the man of knowledge takes the psychotropic substance and gets directly and immediately to his ally.

The personal ally is made of the same matter of the dreams world and its function is to act as a guide and to assist the shaman in his actions, great or small, good or bad.

Ancient shamans all over the world, thanks to the use of the hallucinogenic plants, could enter a non-ordinary reality – separate reality – and develop a transcendental knowledge. Among the shamans of ancient Mexico this knowledge was known with the term of 'nagualism' and it was mainly divided into six groups of two categories each.

Nagualism's secret knowledge

The region of light and the region of darkness, the air and the earth, the fire and the water, above and below, noise and silence, still and moving.

The secret knowledge of the region of light concerns sunlight, the Sun, the day. It is about the mysteries related to organic life.

The region of light's counterpart is known as region of darkness and concerns moonlight, the Moon, the night. It is about the mysteries related to entities without organic life.

The secret knowledge of air concerns the power of the four winds which is represented by the four kinds of women. The woman of persevering will-power is the east wind, the warm temperate morning wind. Then there's the woman of lustful power which is the south wind, the warm wind of the day. Then follows the woman of mysterious power which is the west wind, the cold temperate evening wind. Finally there's the woman of strong power which is the north wind, the cold wind of the night.

The air's counterpart is the secret knowledge of earth. It concerns a deep knowledge of spells – made up of words, gestures and symbols – which are thrown on the man for his preservation or destruction. It furthermore concerns some animals and insects by means of which unguents for curative or destructive purpose are made. It concerns also the use of the roots of trees and plants to obtain potions in order to cure, to make someone ill and to generate altered perception states. Finally, it concerns the use of stones as means to transfer one's personal power.

The secret knowledge of fire and air has to do with their properties, one superior and one inferior. Fire's superior property is the flame and the inferior one is the heat. For water, its superior property is the fluid and the inferior one is the wet. Fire's flame and water's fluid are the means to carry the shamans – in their magical bodies – to the inorganic life's kingdom. Fire's heat and water's wet are considered as minor properties.

The secret knowledge of above concerns clouds, rain, lightning, flashes and thunders, whereas the below concerns fog, underground springs water, bogs and earthquakes.

Noise and silence's secret knowledge concerns sounds and silence's manipulation. Finally, the still and the moving concern particular practices which deal with specific aspects of movement and immobility.

In Nagualism, 'to see' the world in another way represents the higher goal. Besides looking – the usual way we are used to perceive the world – the ancient shamans developed the *seeing*, the capability to perceive the essence – proto-energy – of the things of the world. Thanks to the *seeing* they became expert seers able to perceive the proto-energy as it flows in the universe in form of luminous filaments, and human being's proto-energy like a white bubble, opaque, on which shines a spot of intense brightness – *assemblage point* – which regulates the perception. With millenniums elapsing their *seeing* became so refined to be able to classify the reality and thus they outlined the 'perception map', the 'magical way' of Quetzalcoatl, the 'secret knowledge' of the Feathered Serpent.

The map of perception

The Eagle and its emanations

The Spirit that rules and is at the origins of life is a field of force – proto-energy – of immense proportions called Eagle, since it's seen as an enormous black and white eagle made of luminous and dark primordial energy. And the Eagle, eternal and immutable, spreads in the universe a ceaseless flow of fluid emanations, fixed fibers – rays – made of aware, vibrant and luminous filaments. They are always gathered in groups and the groups are called "big bands of emanations". These groups are made up of billions of filaments that appear straight and don't wave like the other energies in the universe.

The forty-eight big bands of emanations

The Earth is passed thru by forty-eight big bands of emanations that merge around it, forming an enormous bubble of proto-energy in spherical shape. These bands produce containers full of emanations, but only eight of them produce containers with awareness.

One of the forty-eight big bands of emanations – the very big band – produces bubbles of proto-energy related to organic and inorganic life, seven of them produce bubbles correlated to the inorganic life and the remaining forty are associated only to the structure. The very big band of emanations is made up of four Attentions: the Domain (First Attention) and the three Kingdoms (Second, Third and Fourth Attention). The Kingdom of Attention Zero, being fused with the Third Attention, displays inorganic life with bubbles of gloomy proto-energy, defined as "alien" because it differs, by nature, from proto-energy.

In the very big organic and inorganic band there are organic beings which have shells, cocoons and globes with awareness and inorganic entities having receptacles with awareness. In the other seven big inorganic bands are present only inorganic entities owning receptacles with awareness. And the product of the remaining forty bands is given by configurations of inanimate energy called containers (pots), because they are without awareness.

The Domain and the Four inorganic Kingdoms

In the Domain, exists the man (human kingdom) and other forms of organic life (animal and vegetable kingdom) and inorganic life (mineral kingdom).

In the mineral kingdom, minerals have a bubble of proto-energy in the shape of a pot, they are not aware and don't own the *assemblage point*, the point which regulates perception.

In the vegetable kingdom, plants have a bubble of proto-energy in the shape of a shell, they are aware and their *assemblage point* is situated very low, related to the genital center.

In the animal kingdom, animals have a bubble of proto-energy in the shape of a cocoon, they are conscious and their *assemblage point* is placed in correspondence of the umbilical center.

In the human kingdom, terrestrials have a sphere-shaped bubble of proto-energy, they are conscious and their *assemblage point* is positioned in correspondence of the cardiac center.

In the four inorganic Kingdoms exist only inorganic entities. They have a bubble of proto-energy in the shape of a receptacle, they are aware and their *assemblage point*, which hasn't the peculiarities of that one of the man, is located according to the kind of entity.

Forms of light

In the bubble of Earth there are models of proto-energy – forms of light – which are of use to imprint specific qualities on bubbles which merge different living beings. Each species has its form of light – mold and matrix – and each single form of life shows characteristic features specific of its species.

The mold of the man is a gigantic static image which groups a particular band of luminous fibers. This beam of light is related to organic life and appears as a bright amber light. It is the prototype of the man, his source, his origin.

Emanations' alignment

All living beings, like Earth, are contained in bubbles of proto-energy made up of the same filaments of Eagle's emanations, and the filaments contained in the man's bubble are the same present in the bubble of Earth. And all the bands of emanations passing thru Earth are found again, in a small scale, in man's bubble's composition, and its internal emanations are aligned with the external ones.

The alignment of emanations existing between the man and the Earth allows the shaman to use it like a push that helps the *assemblage point* to move and to perceive the four inorganic Kingdoms. Therefore, the *assemblage point* is the secret passage and the key is the push of Earth.

Emanations' energy

In Eagle's emanations there is an energy, called "strength-will", which appears in two aspects: the circular aspect (will) and the rotating aspect (strength). And the Eagle gives life thru the circular strength which appears as iridescent azure rings, whereas it gives death thru the rotating strength which appears as globes of fire. These two strengths hit ceaselessly the proto-energy bubbles of all living beings and when the rotating strength hits them stronger than the circular one the equilibrium is upset ... and death comes. In fact, on man's bubble there is a slit – in correspondence of the navel – that is opened by the rotating strength, at the moment of death; the bubble collapses and the internal emanations, now released, flow flooding it.

Awareness, assemblage point and intent

The Eagle grants awareness – awareness B – to all living beings, organic and inorganic ones. In the moment of conception, the emanations inside the bubbles of the two partners get agitated and two pieces of aware proto-energy, one for each, come off from the bubbles to melt and create a new bubble which receives a new awareness. In fact, the Eagle wants that all living beings enrich awareness thru life experiences and, when death comes, it is reabsorbed with the bubble … the food of the Eagle.

The seers *see* the human being as a white globe with lateral arms, much bigger than a man, similar to a luminous sphere spreading almost as far as a meter from the physical body. This form is a bubble made up of billions of not-lighted filaments, a bubble of proto-energy containing a luminous nucleus – awareness B – which makes the bubble to seem bright, but which actually is opaque. Only a little part of this opaque globe is lighted up by a point of intense splendor – surrounded by a luminous halo – located inside the bubble, on the surface, at about fifty centimeters from the tip of the right shoulder-blade of each person. It's this *assemblage point*, with its bright halo – sign of perception and life – which regulates the human being's perception. Moving, it lights up thousands of filaments inside the bubble that, hence lighted, interact with the external ones, leading to the perception.

The seers *see* the impersonal energy deriving from emanations and they call it "strength-will". This energy is directly responsible of man's perception and, indirectly, of his *assemblage point*'s dislocation. The aspect of the strength-will which keeps the *assemblage point* stationary is the strength, and the aspect that makes it move is the will. When the seers manipulate this kind of energy they call it "power"; so the emanations' impersonal energy turns into *intent*, the personalized energy working for the seer.

The six points on the bubble

On the man's bubble there are six points corresponding to particular zones of the physical body. They are called: "intent" (strength-will), "will", "strength", "hear", "perceive" (or "dreaming") and "seeing".

The *intent* is directly connected to all the other points and it corresponds to the umbilical zone. The *strength* is related to the area under the navel and the *will* to the zone above the navel. Thru these three points *intent* is expressed, an energy emanated from the umbilical region thru an opening on the bubble.

Then there is the *seeing* – *seeing* the proto-energy – which corresponds to the zone of the right hip, the *perceiving* – enter the Attentions – which corresponds to the zone of the left hip and the *hearing* – *hearing intent*'s voice – which is related to the zone of the breast bone's tip.

Inorganic beings

The organic beings live only in the Domain, while the inorganic ones exist in the Domain and in the four inorganic Kingdoms.

In the Domain exist the magical beings (space-time entities) which show themselves with an appearance of animals and insects. They can be perceived thru the *seeing* and the perception's barrier allow these beings' and organic ones' awareness to coexist without hindering each other. The pre-eminently magical being is the power butterfly that, like all the other magical beings, communicates with the man in a subliminal way.

In the Domain there are also the voladores (entities of black proto-energy), bubbles of aware beings who lived on other planets which, after physical death, came on Earth – about thirteen thousand years ago – when the Golden Age ended. Since then, they come on Earth and each individual entity connects to each individual human being thru a tentacle that it inserts in the individual's bubble – in correspondence of the navel – at the moment of his birth. The voladores live on the shining coating that wraps the man's bubble, consuming it so much that they reduce it to a thin border when the individual comes of adult age. At that point, they stimulate the remaining thin band to make it produce proto-energetic blazes that then they continue to consume. In order to produce and stoke these blazes they influence the man's mind taking advantage of his self-centeredness, causing him futile problems, contradicting behaviors and an aberrant system of beliefs.

In the four inorganic Kingdoms there are the allies (space-time and time entities) which can take on various appearances, humane form included. They are perceivable thru the *seeing* and the perception's barrier prevents organic beings from getting in touch with them. The shamans, instead, have the ability to penetrate the perception's barrier, to enter the Attentions, to get in touch with the allies and draw them into the First Attention. Thus, they can entrust the allies with tasks, so that the ancient sorcerers considered them as their servants, but they made the mistake to give to the *inorganic beings* the power to break the barrier of perception of human beings' First Attention.

In the fourth inorganic Kingdom there are also the parallel beings (time entities), the counterparts of the organic beings. They are entities of the same sex of their own counterparts, deeply and inextricably linked to them. The organic beings who can meet their own parallel beings can find an unlimited source of energy in them.

In the sphere of don Juan's secret knowledge we can distinguish quite five areas in which perception can be extended: the known, the unknown, the almost untold unknown, the untold unknown and the unknowable.

The known is what we can normally perceive and that is about the First Attention. It corresponds to the awareness A that each person has developed as living being, and it comprises the physical body's awareness.

In order to perceive the known, the man's *assemblage point* makes particular filaments, located at the right side of the bubble, to shine, on a narrow vertical band flowing all along the bubble, the man's amber band. It can *vary* its position, that is to say it can *change* it making a *modification* inside the organic part of the big human band (organic-inorganic).

The unknown – human unknown – is what is concealed but within human being's grasp and concerns the Second Attention, the Third Attention, Attention Zero and the Fourth Attention.

They correspond to the awareness B one needs to take on one's magical bodies and, thanks to the push of Earth, to enter the four inorganic Kingdoms.

To perceive the unknown, the man's *assemblage point* makes shine rejected filaments, inside the big human band existing in the bubble. It can *vary* its position, that is it can *shift* making a *movement* towards the inorganic part of the big human band (organic-inorganic).

The almost untold unknown – not human unknown – is what is concealed but still within human being's grasp and it concerns the seven inorganic bands. They correspond to the awareness B that one needs in order to take on one's magical bodies and, thanks to the push of the rotating strength, to enter the seven inorganic worlds.

To perceive the almost untold unknown, the man's *assemblage point* makes shine the filaments on the outside of the big human band present in bubble. It can *transfer* its position, that is to say it can *rectify* it making a *removal*, shifting towards the seven inorganic bands.

The untold unknown – not human unknown – is what is concealed and almost out of human being's reach, and it's about the mere form's forty bands. They correspond to emanations' awareness, and awareness B is needed to take on magical bodies and enter the mere form's forty worlds.

In order to perceive the untold unknown, the man's *assemblage point* makes shine the filaments outside the big human band present in the bubble. It can *transfer* its position, that is to say it can *rectify* it making a *removal*, shifting towards the forty world of mere form.

The unknowable is what cannot be comprehended and not within the human being's grasp and it concerns the Fifth Attention. It corresponds to the awareness B needed to perceive one's own proto-energy bubble and to act as magical men.

To perceive – *see* – the unknowable, the man's *assemblage point* makes shine the filaments inside the big human band present in the bubble. It can *vary* its position, that is it can *shift* making a *movement* towards the inorganic part of the big human band (organic-inorganic).

To comprehend the unknowable, the man's *assemblage point* must light up all the filaments inside the bubble, since the whole bubble is made of proto-energy and it is the unknowable.

Still in the sphere of don Juan's secret knowledge two terms are used to mean that an organic reality – *tonal* – and an unknown inorganic reality – *nagual* – exist. There are the space *tonal*, the known world, and the space *nagual*, the inorganic worlds; the time *tonal*, the human community, and the time *nagual*, the inorganic community; the personal *tonal*, the organic individual, and the personal *nagual*, the inorganic entity.

Furthermore, inside the man – personal *tonal* – there are two sides, two counterparts which activate at the moment of the birth: one is called *tonal*, the awareness A, and the other is called *nagual*, the awareness B. Awareness B comes soon into effect but then, in order to work, awareness A is needed and it becomes ruling darkening awareness B. Ever since we completely develop awareness A we intuit that two sides exist in us and we feel incomplete.

The shamans only – men of knowledge – can re-establish the direct contact with their own awareness B, very conscious of the dramatic situation in which the human being is, whose mind is under a double influence: that one of voladores – black proto-energy entities – which bring arrogance, doubt and despair, and that of awareness B, which rarely speaks and brings order and direction. Sometimes, under this double influence, the mind becomes inconsistent, the result of the conflict between the voladores and the awareness B.

In living beings, awareness A – given by life experiences – is memorized in awareness B which enriches, and only in the shaman awareness B communicates with the mind and enables awareness A to spread.

In the man, the totality of being is a bunch of perception – perception bubble – made up of two parts, the right side and the left side. Half of the totality is the ultimate center of "reason" and the second half is the ultimate center of "learning". Reason is the intellectual power thru which man knows, judges and rules himself, whereas learning allow to know without knowing, the silent knowledge without words beyond the power of understanding.

Reason is indirectly connected to learning thru intuition, while learning is directly linked to hearing.

Intuition is the prompt comprehension, the intuitive flash; whereas hearing is a vague but familiar feeling, a particular feeling of learning … is knowing something without any doubt.

The teacher turns to both sides of the apprentice's totality and to do this he gives him to know the "way of the warrior" – the warrior's path or the warrior behavior – which allows him to develop harmoniously a perfect balance between reason and learning, since without this balance it's not possible to hold out on the way of learning and power.

The teacher's task – he instructs giving explanations – consists of inducing the apprentice to clean up the left half of the bubble – perception – of his elements on the side of learning, and of leading him to group and set all his elements in order in the right half of the bubble on the reason's side.

The benefactor's task – he instructs without giving explanations – consists of opening the warrior's bubble on the side where it has been cleaned – that one of learning – in order that he may spread the wings of perception, that is he may enlarge a little his bunch of single feelings nevertheless without the bunch losing its unity by disintegrating. Thus the warrior has a look at his being's totality and comprehends that it is a bunch of unified single perceptions.

When don Juan came to me – with his inorganic body – to give me Nagualism's *secret teachings* he revealed me, while I was in a silent perception state, that I was a particular Nagual, since I had a special proto-energetic configuration.

The term Nagual designates the chief of a group of warriors

– Nagual's followers – and a person endowed with an extraordinary energy, in fact the common men has a proto-energy bubble divided into two parts, while three-forked Naguals have a three-sided bubble and four-forked Naguals have a four-sided one.

Then don Juan revealed me the secret part of the four-forked Nagual's rule and the secret part of the three-forked Nagual's rule.

Four-forked Nagual's rule

The Eagle gives the four-forked Nagual (he appears as a pair, male and female), as companions, four she-*stalker* warriors, three *stalker* warriors and a messenger. Moreover, it gives him the task to find four other she-*dreamer* warriors, three *dreamer* warriors and a messenger.

Stalker-women – like *dreamer* ones too – are named the four directions, the four winds, the four different female personalities existing in human race.

The first one is the east. She's called Order. She represents the warm temperate wind, the morning wind which brings light. Her personality is gay, sweet and persevering like a strong breeze.

The second one is the south. Her name is Growth. She represents the afternoon wing blowing full of energy. Her personality is happy, carefree and hot like a torrid wind.

The third one is the west. Her name is Strength. She represents the cold temperate wind, the evening wind which protects and wraps everything. Her personality is impatient, pure and tenacious like an impetuous wind.

The fourth one is the north. She's called Feeling. She represents the night wind that freezes and makes weeping. Her personality is malicious, pensive and shrewd like a cold wind gust.

Stalker-men – like the *dreamer* ones too – represent the

four directions, the four kinds of male activity and temperament.

The first one is the east. He's the scholar, totally busy in the accomplishment of his duty.

The second one is the north. He's a man of action, inconstant and amusing.

The third one is the west. He's a man who plots behind the scenes, impenetrable and mysterious.

The fourth is the south. He's the assistant, dark and mysterious.

So people under a four-forked Nagual's guidance are in the number of sixteen: eight she-warriors, six warriors and two messengers. Added to the Nagual man and the Nagual woman they are eighteen in all.

Three-forked Nagual's rule

The Eagle gives the three-forked Nagual (he appears as a pair, male and female), as companions, three she-*dreamer* warriors, two *dreamer* warriors and a messenger. Furthermore, it gives him the task to find three other she-*stalker* warriors, two *stalker* warriors and a messenger.

Dreamer women – like *stalkers* ones too – are named the four directions, the four winds, the four different female personalities existing in human race.

The first one is the west, the second one is the north, the third one is the east and the fourth one is the south. The three-forked Nagual woman represents the south and she's the foster-mother woman.

Dreamer men – like *stalker* ones too – represent the four directions, the four kinds of male activity and temperament.

The first one is the west, the second one is the south, the third one is the east and the fourth one is the north. The three-forked Nagual man represents the north and is the man of action.

So people under a three-forked Nagual's guidance are in the number of twelve: six she-warriors, four warriors and two messengers. Added to the Nagual man and the Nagual woman they are fourteen in all.

2

The way of the warrior

The magic is a magical bird, “the bird of Freedom”. This bird breaks his flight for a moment in order to enable the man to follow the way of learning and of power, but if the man is irresolute the bird flies away and it never comes back again. If the man, instead, is determined to follow the way of the warrior he must do it in the right way: he must be watchful, must have respect and proceed with awe and absolute firmness.

The way of the warrior essentially teaches how to assume behaviors that allow to face the world intelligently. The individual, in practice, interacting with the environment, changes his behaviors and reactions and thus he renews his existence, that is he molds his life’s directions and consequences, but to do this he has continuously to review the teachings he has been given, since only in this way he’ll be able to apply them to his everyday life.

Furthermore, the warrior reuses his energy in an intelligent way. In practice, he lists his own interests – strategic inventories – and removes those that are not essential for his well-being and in this way he gets a pause in his energy’s consumption. Then, when he becomes a man of knowledge, he develops the *unbending intent*, a punctiliously well defined thought, he overcomes the personal importance – conceit – that consumes most of his energy and obtains the inner strength, that is he attains sobriety, a natural inclination for analysis and comprehension.

Finally, the man of knowledge uses energy rightly – he re-canalizes energy to face the unknown – and such an action is impeccability; his sobriety allows him to become a seer which controls his own *intent* – he moves and fixes the *assemblage point* – and connects himself with the great tyrant, the Eagle. He's rational, methodic, analytic and, at the same time, he refuses these qualities in order to be free and open to the mysteries of existence.

When a man is ready to be given knowledge – whether he likes it or not – he crosses the "threshold of infinity" and the *power* provides him a teacher. Since then the course of his life is ruled by *intent*, the active aspect of *infinity*. So he becomes an apprentice and the teacher instructs him on a both theoretical and practical level, giving him all necessary explanations. Opposite, the apprentice must trust the teacher completely and wholeheartedly accept him as his guide – Nagual – and to do this he must cede his individuality.

The first natural enemy

When an apprentice starts his way of learning and of power he begins being frightened, since knowledge implies having to face unknown and unknown terrifies. And so he bumped into his first natural enemy: Fear.

To overcome fear, the apprentice must challenge it constantly and to do this he must keep learning, until his fear becomes absolute. Still he must not give up and the moment when his enemy will be defeated will come.

The apprentice, while he follows the way of the warrior, gets the right way of thinking and assumes the right way of behaving. He never deems to know because knowledge is endless and, in his acting, he's free from invasive expectations, fears of failure, hopes of success.

Apprentice's attributes

When a man becomes apprentice he begins getting a systematic control of his behavior by means of four attributes: logic, order, care and respect.

The first attribute of the apprentice is logic, which conforms to reason.

An apprentice, in order to improve his logic, must make the correct reasoning, that is to say he has to develop his thoughts in a simple and linear way. In this way he'll become a thinker whose talent is reason's exercise.

The second attribute of the apprentice is order.

The apprentice, to estimate his own order, must see how to place things and to improve it he has to place them with the greatest logic. This will allow him to improve his inner order, which will be reflected on the outer one.

The third attribute of the apprentice is care.

The apprentice, to achieve a better care, must develop a watchful care of himself. Only in this way he'll develop a better care to the fellow human being.

The fourth attribute of the apprentice is respect.

The apprentice, to attain the right respect, must analyze himself, to take note of what he is and accept himself. This will allow him to have a balanced respect towards himself and to show a correct respect towards other people. Thus the right respect will come towards the world around him, nature.

With the other four attributes, the teacher will submit to the apprentice two practical tasks.

The tasks of the apprentice

The first task submitted to the apprentice is known as "the right way of walking".

The apprentice must take on a fluent gait, his walk must be light, harmonious and linear.

The second task submitted to the apprentice is known as "acting just for acting and being efficient".

The apprentice must be humble and efficient: he must act without expecting anything in exchange and must cope with anything it could occur. His love for knowledge must have as ultimate aim knowledge itself – every deviation from this principle implies to fall in the yearning of the result – and his dedication must be absolute because only in this way he can cope with any situation.

The apprentice, after he has achieved the four attributes and carried out the two tasks, is ready to tune in with everything around him, receiving approvals. He becomes aware that, in his talking and acting, the world sends him signals that corroborate what he's saying and doing.

At this point, the teacher resorts to a clever trick, inventing a subtle trap. To carry out this he uses the worthy adversary who can be one of his allies or a warrior his accomplice. The clash between the apprentice and the worthy adversary – who is not an enemy – can totally change the apprentice or destroy him.

The trap allows the teacher to hold the apprentice, compelling him to choose between the magical world and the earthly world. Only by deception the apprentice can be driven on the way of learning and of power and, of course, the teacher will do his best in order that the apprentice may choose the world and the life of the warrior.

After the apprentice has overcome the clash with the worthy adversary, the teacher imposes him a practical task, a sort of difficult situation. This situation must be appropriate to the apprentice's personality and must damage his image in the world.

Finally, the apprentice is ready to become a warrior and the teacher keeps instructing him on a theoretical and practical level. Furthermore, the *power* provides the apprentice with a benefactor who, by means of the art of *stalking*, puts him into direct contact with the unknown, without giving any explanation.

The second natural enemy

The apprentice starts feeling self-confident and becomes a warrior lucidly aware of his learning. And thus he meets his second natural enemy: Lucidity.

To overcome lucidity the warrior must challenge it and to do this he must comprehend that all his learning is only a little fragment of the universal knowledge. In this way he'll have defeated his second enemy.

The warrior is a humble being because he puts all human beings on the same level and is unblemished, that is he does his best in his acting. He must be fluent in order to interact harmoniously with everything around him, since only by living as a warrior he can hold out on the way of learning and of power. Therefore, he cannot be powerless, bewildered or frightened, since this would lead him to impoverish his energy.

The attributes of the warrior

When a man becomes a warrior he proceeds in his behavior's systematic control by means of six other attributes: control, discipline, detachment, decisiveness, balance and astuteness.

The first attribute of the warrior is control.

The warrior, to achieve control, must be calm and have self-control.

The second attribute of the warrior is discipline.

The warrior, in order to become a disciplined man, must regulate in a harmonious way the course of his existence and must develop the ability to face the unknown in a serene way, without vacillating, but to do this he must be inspired by awe.

The third attribute of the warrior is detachment.

The warrior, to achieve detachment, must lose his *human form* that allows him to become a shapeless warrior. He gives up his attachment to things and people, becomes without prejudices and a strange peace becomes the leading strength of his existence.

The fourth attribute of the warrior is decisiveness.

The warrior, to display the power of his decisions, must be the master of his choices, he must think before deciding and when he has decided he has no time left for regrets and recriminations, since his decisions are definitive.

The fifth attribute of the warrior is balance.

The warrior, to reach his inner balance, must be able to analyze his being and must be capable to judge correctly his own actions, in order to be able to act impeccably.

The sixth attribute of the warrior is astuteness.

The warrior, in order to achieve astuteness, must be able to plan his actions with cool determination. This will allow him to behave, according to the situations, in the most effective and incisive way. So his acts will always be refined, since told by his style and his elegance.

The warrior has the duty to protect himself – not to defend – and so he reduces any risk to a minimum, since he's aware of his great fortune; he knows that to be destined to the learning of the men of knowledge is part of *power*'s plans and, thus, he considers everything like a challenge – a common man considers everything like a blessing or a misfortune – and regrets nothing or complains about nothing, but above all he surrenders to nothing, not even before his death. He considers himself as already dead – he knows that death is the unchangeable destiny of the man – and knows that he has nothing to lose in accepting the great challenge that *infinity* asks him, to defeat death and find Freedom.

The warrior's nine steps

A man – apprentice – to become a warrior-*stalker* must accomplish nine steps.

The first step of the warrior consists of breaking one's life habits.

The warrior must not be bound to his habits, but he must be fluent and unpredictable.

The second step of the warrior consists of taking the death as an adviser.

The common man lives as if death would never touch him and, therefore, he has no awareness of his death. Instead, a man who follows the way of the warrior finds death at each street corner and thus he becomes aware of its presence. So he realizes that death is his irreplaceable companion, always beside him, the eternal adviser always watching over him and bearing witness of everything he does. Thus he understands that nothing matters except the touch of his death and that the day when he'll be touched will come. But the thought of his impending death must not obsess him – to worry about his death would weaken him – and thus he must react with indifference.

The third step of the warrior consists of searching the perfection of being, the only worthy aim of his man's nature.

The warrior, in order to find the perfection of being, must always and in any case act in the warrior's frame of mind, state in which one doesn't feel hurt by the fellow human beings' acts.

The fourth step of the warrior consists of assuming the responsibility of his own decisions.

The warrior must assume the responsibility of everything he does. First of all he must know why he does it, then he must carry on his actions without any doubt, ready to die for his own decisions.

The fifth step of the warrior consists of putting himself in balance with the world and to do this he must be unapproachable.

The warrior, in order to put himself in balance with the world around him, must be a skillful strategist and must know when the right moment to act is or not. Thus he doesn't leave anything to chance and affects on events' outcome with his awareness and his will-power. Furthermore, he must assess his talk and his doing, in order not to exhaust himself and other people.

The sixth step of the warrior consists of aging so as each act is that last battle on Earth.

The warrior assesses each act carefully and carries it out doing his very best. With the thought of his impending death he makes himself completely aware not to have time and so each act is his last battle.

The seventh step of the warrior consists of having to believe.

The warrior, in front of events he cannot verify, chooses to believe according to his predilection. He does not believe, he must believe.

The eighth step of the warrior consists of getting rid of the burden to feel indebted and of saying thanks.

The warrior, just before throwing himself in the unknown, pays each favor he has been given with style and generosity in order to free himself of the burden to be indebted. Then he thanks all those who have loved him. With the *intent* coming from his obscurity – deep silence – he says thanks and thus he keeps inside everything he has loved.

The ninth step of the warrior consists of loving the Earth.

The warrior concentrates all his love on that being that accommodates him, Mother Earth... and Earth, that knows to be loved, grants him its protection. This is the warrior's innermost predilection which saturates him with joy and donates him freedom.

At this point the warrior has come to the end of his apprenticeship and the teacher sums up – formal reconsideration – all the steps done to make knowledge lasting. Now he's ready to become a man of knowledge who, without hurrying and without hesitating, reveals the secrets of learning and of power. Despite his precariousness, that is his tiredness and his impending death, he goes on along the "way which has a heart", finding satisfaction and personal fulfillment in what he does. He's a fluent, malleable and very resourceful being, which has an iron will – *unbending intent* – and which has an ally who is at his service, the personal ally.

The third, the fourth and the fifth natural enemy

The warrior starts feeling that he has self-control and becomes a man of knowledge who can have power at his disposal as he wishes. And thus he meets his third natural enemy: Power.

If the warrior succumbs to power he becomes a sorcerer, a cruel and capricious man who's no longer able to control himself and his power.

To overcome power, the man of knowledge must challenge it and to do it he must comprehend that the power he achieved must be controlled and, in this way, he'll understand how and when to use it. In this way he'll be able to have everything under control without controlling anything and he'll have overcome his third enemy.

At this point, the man of knowledge starts feeling tired, he feels the irresistible longing to rest. And thus he meets his fourth natural enemy: Tiredness.

To overcome tiredness the man of knowledge must not surrender to it, but he must free himself from its influence. In this way he'll have overcome his fourth enemy.

At his point the man of knowledge meets the last of his enemies: Death.

This enemy is the most to be feared of all, the only one that cannot be totally defeated, but only chased away.

To overcome death the man of knowledge must face it and to do this he must survive its attack.

The man of knowledge never wastes his personal power – energetic supercharging – and goes unnoticed. He has no time to lose for mean conflicts and the only authentic conflict occurs inside him, and when he overcomes it he becomes a man whose inner self reflects *infinity*, since he has emptied himself – breaking the reflection of oneself – overcoming his individual inner self (ego). So he keeps nothing for himself and devotes himself totally to what he has in front of him… and to do it he's always on the alert, that is he's always aware of the plot lying behind the events of the moment.

The attributes of the man of knowledge

When a warrior becomes a man of knowledge he proceeds in his behavior's systematic control by means of five other attributes: patience, kindness, indifference, sense of timing and pitilessness.

The first attribute of the man of knowledge is patience.

The man of knowledge, in order to acquire patience, waits for his aim's achievement taking it easy, without hurry and without anguish.

The second attribute of the man of knowledge is kindness.

The man of knowledge, to acquire kindness, must be harmony-hearted, but must act with firmness and gentleness.

The third attribute of the man of knowledge is indifference.

The man of knowledge, to achieve indifference, facing unusual life's situations, behaves as if nothing happened, even if he's feared. His self-domain is faultless.

The fourth attribute of the man of knowledge is the sense of timing.

The man of knowledge, in order to achieve the sense of timing, must be able to seize the right moment when he can act.

The fifth attribute of the man of knowledge is pitilessness.

The man of knowledge, to acquire pitilessness, must lose his conceit, that is he must throw away his personal importance. So he achieves pitilessness, which is not ferocity but sobriety.

The man of knowledge knows that his challenge is how much he can be impeccable in his destiny's immutability and he knows that Freedom's quest is the only stimulating power, an adventure in which he's risking his life.

He knows that Freedom's achievement can be attained only facing *infinity*.

The man of knowledge's six steps

The first step of the man of knowledge consists of making himself accessible to the *power*.

The man of knowledge becomes accessible to the *power* when he perceives an uncontrollable energy running him over. This energy stimulates him making his interior power to emerge – an itch and a heat are perceived in the umbilical zone; then a pain and a sense of sickness – and always this energy controls his acts and, at the same time, obeys his orders.

The second step of the man of knowledge consists of taking on a particular way of running in the dark of the night, a way known as “the walk of power”.

The man of knowledge assumes a gait in which the spine is erect but the trunk is a little bent forward and the knees are slightly bent. The arms are stretched out along the hips and the hand’s fingers are bent against the palm with stretched thumbs and forefingers. The eyes are fixed on the ground ahead and each step lifts the knees almost up to the chest, so that the steps can be very short and sure. In this way he lets flow, inside him, his own personal power so that it may merge with the power of the night.

The third step of the man of knowledge consists of undertaking battles of power.

The man of knowledge is an impeccable *stalker* which entraps the *power* and accumulates it. When he entraps the *power*, he perceives it as a sensation he feels for certain things and, when he accumulates it, he perceives it as another sensation depending on his natural inclination. *Power*’s accumulation allows him to increase his personal power, up to the moment when he’ll be able to engage his first battle of power, his direct contact with the unknown.

The fourth step of the man of knowledge consists of performing the power’s dance.

When the man of knowledge is touched by death he performs the dance of power, that is he re-evokes the story of his life – *recapitulation* – and the death stops until he has finished. Then it takes him and so the man will have performed his last dance of power. But if he has acquired an impeccable form – dance – of power the death refuses him, since he has developed an impeccable movement – dance – of power throughout his life, a movement that has grown with his personal power’s growing and that is performed under the influence of this power. The death, refusing the man of knowledge, allows him to realize the symbolic but definitive death and thus he invalidates his old existence’s continuity. This is the ticket to impeccability – the ticket to freedom – that allows him to utilize intelligently – to act in complete safety –

his new continuity.

The fifth step of the man of knowledge consists of losing conceit.

The man of knowledge admits that conceit – personal importance – is the force generated by the individual self (ego), one self's reflection or image. He furthermore comprehends that self-commiseration – to feel sorry for oneself – is the propulsive force that increases the personal importance and, if he removes the pity for himself, thru his symbolic but definitive death, he loses conceit and acquires pitilessness (sobriety).

The sixth step of the man of knowledge consists of deleting his personal story.

The man of knowledge must wish to renounce his personal story in order to break the bonds of the thoughts of all those who know him. Only in this way he rids himself of the ties of other people's thoughts. He must start deleting his personal story, cutting it off little by little, until the moment in which nobody knows who he is, neither himself. Then he must delete everything around him till when he takes nothing more for granted and thus he always remains attentive, everlastingly active.

At this point the man of knowledge has overcome death – it cannot be totally defeated but only chased away – which acknowledges its defeat and does not challenge him anymore. He has broken his perceptive barriers – the leap of the thought into the inconceivable – and human perception has reached its limits. Furthermore, he has broken the chains of the reflection of himself – personal importance – and this allows him not to share people's worries and problems anymore. He keeps staying in everyday world but is no more part of it.

The attribute of the seer

When the man of knowledge becomes a seer he must

master an attribute: *intent*.

The seer, in order to master *intent*, must interact with the Eagle, the great tyrant.

The seer does not fear evil – mere lucubration of the mind – because he knows that in the universe exists only the energy. For him, what is of importance is the personal power and his ability to use his own *intent*, and the only thing he fears is to lose his connection with *infinity*.

The seer's step

The step of the seer consists of *stopping the world*.

The seer, in order to *stop the world*, must stop watching – doing – to make emerge the *seeing* – *not doing* – by means of the technique of contemplation. To put this technique into effect the contemplator gazes at the objects and keeps his eyes half-closed. In this way the thoughts calm down till to come to the interruption of their flow – interruption of the inner dialogue – and in this way the inner silence is achieved. At this point the ordinary perception collapses – *stopping the world* – and appears an extraordinary perception, the *seeing*.

The man who follows the way of the warrior knows that, despite all the acquired knowledge and wisdom it's impossible to help other people because to help would mean to do an arbitrary act told only by egoism. Therefore he has no compassion for anyone, since having compassion would mean to wish the others equal to him. Moreover, while he follows the 'way', he's aware that sadness and the universal joy he feels are not a personal matter but an influence of the dark and bright side of *infinity*, waves of energy coming from the depths of the universe and hitting him when he's more receptive. He knows he cannot hide behind anything and anyone and while he waits for conquer Freedom – his ultimate state – he watches the magnificence of nature, the great show of the world, and in doing it he feels joy, the frame of mind that reflects his supreme perfection.

3

The art of *stalking*

The ancient seer shamans realized that each strange behavior produced a tremble in the *assemblage point* and soon they found that each unusual behavior systematically kept made the *assemblage point* to move in a slow but constant way. Then they decided to put at right a particular behavioral system that, still, would combine ethics with the sense of aesthetics and, thus, they developed the most mysterious of the magic arts, the art of *stalking*.

The art of *stalking* is essentially based on the behavior's systematic control which produces a movement leftwards of the *stalker*'s *assemblage point*. This allows activating some internal filaments, usually never used, in the proto-energy bubble, widening awareness and perception.

The shamans learn the *stalking* while they are in the normal perception state and apply it – *controlled folly* – when they are in the high perception state – the intense perception state's precursor – because it allows acting quicker in the *stalking* accomplishment.

When don Juan came to me – with his inorganic body – he told me, while I was in the silent perception state, that he was a *stalker* and that his art was that of *stalking*.

Don Juan, to start me in *stalking*, taught me to become a

stalking stalker able to capture my own faults – bad habits – and to remove them. He explained to me that first of all I had to recognize them, then I had to know each aspect they were made up of and, finally, I had to devise a strategy that would allow their demolition. In order to help me to demolish my faults, he told me that each habit is a "live activity", a "doing", a repeated action which consolidates as time passes and that I had to insert some dissonant elements in the tissue they were made up of, in order to interfere in the "doing flow", till the moment of the death of habit.

In the following meetings he made me to experiment the inner First Attention – to wake up in the inner *tonal* with the inner physical body – that is one of the perceptive faculty of the *stalking stalkers* and he gave me very precise instructions about the practical task that is submitted to the warrior-*stalker*, task known as "the recapitulation".

The shamans of ancient times gave orally their teaching to the disciples and in order not to forget what they had taught they recapitulated – formal reconsideration – all they had told and done. Similarly, the disciples, to remember what they had learned, did the same.

After that, the ancient seer shamans noticed the power of the *recapitulation*. They realized that it caused a light but constant movement of the *assemblage point* and took to the surface all the litter of one's life, that is it freed all the feelings of great importance such as hopes, fears and so on.

The first way of proceeding in order to carry out the *recapitulation* is formal and strict and is divided into two stages.

The first stage consists of drafting a list of all people known and of all events to be remembered, starting from the present till the beginning of one's existence.

The second stage consists of shutting oneself up in a closet – it reduces the stimulation area around the physical body – and of 'reorganizing' in the mind the last event occurred. To reorganize means to reconstruct the episode in the least details, trying to 'relive' – it causes a slow but constant movement of the *assemblage point* – the feelings and the sensations experienced.

The *stalker* carries out the *recapitulation* combining it with a specific respiratory technique. Long and slow inhalations are made, turning the head slowly from right to left in a 180 degrees arc. After inhaling, the head turns from left to right in a 90 degrees arc. Then, slowly, exhalation is made looking ahead. Finally the head is turned for 90 degrees, till to come at the starting point to begin the cycle again.

The man's proto-energy bubble continually creates filaments similar to spider's webs which are pushed out from the feelings of great importance. And the magic of breathing has a double purpose: to inhale, while an episode is emotionally 'relived', allows to get back the filaments that had been left behind during the interaction, and to exhale allows expelling the filaments that other people had left inside the bubble during the interaction.

The formal *recapitulation,* since it takes to the surface all the litter of one's life, creates inside the disciple the required space suitable to contain all everything has to be known about Nagualism. And the shaman, to convey all his learning, must compress the time, that is he must give his teaching to the disciple on two levels: the teachings transmitted in the normal perception state and the teachings transmitted in the intense perception state.

The second teachings are registered in the intense perception area by means of the shift of the *stalker*'s *assemblage point.* Then the *stalker* returns to the normal perception and does not remember anything anymore. Only later, losing the *human form,* the memories begin to emerge again and the teachings received are recovered, making the *assemblage point* to shift back in the intense perception's specific area. In this way it's possible to re-unite the knowledge received in the normal perception state and in the intense perception state.

The formal *recapitulation*, since it's strict, is the most appropriate system to lose the *human form* and this, in its turn, is the only means to begin remembering. This is possible because the *assemblage point* of the warrior shifts a little leftwards in the position known as "sharp reason". It's a permanent *change*, a *modification* inside the organic part of the big human band which causes the loss of energetic cohesion (*human form*). Furthermore, the *change* has as result the mutation of the former energetic form, in fact the bubble from a spherical form turns into an oval form.

The shamans know that at the basis of the art of *stalking* there are three precepts that constitute the rule of *stalking*.

The three precepts of *stalking*

The first precept of the rule of *stalking* tells that everything around the man is an inscrutable mystery.

The second precept of the rule of *stalking* tells that mysteries must be tried to be revealed, but without hoping to succeed.

The third precept of the rule of *stalking* tells that the *stalker*, aware of the inscrutable mysteries around him, takes his proper place among the other mysteries and considers himself one of them.

It follows that, to a warrior-*stalker*, the being is an endless mystery, either it would be a plant, or an animal or himself. This is the humility of the warrior.

The shamans know that the *stalkers* must learn seven principles to achieve perfection in the art of *stalking*.

The seven principles of *stalking*

The first principle of the art of *stalking* tells that it's up to the *stalker* to decide on what field to clash. A *stalker* never accepts the challenge without knowing what there's around him.

The second principle of the art of *stalking* tells that the *stalker* must discard everything that is not necessary, that is he must get rid of the surplus.

The third principle of the art of *stalking* tells that the *stalker* must be able to decide if a clash has to be accepted or not. Furthermore, he must always be ready to fight to the end, but never without a pre-established plan.

The fourth principle of the art of *stalking* tells that the *stalker* must relax and be frightened of nothing. Only at that moment the *intent* which guides him will open the way and will help him.

The fifth principle of the art of *stalking* tells that the *stalker*, when he finds himself facing situations he cannot control, retires for a moment and let his thoughts to wander, spending his time with something else.

The sixth principle of the art of *stalking* tells that the *stalker* compresses the time, because even an instant has its importance and so he does not even waste a moment.

The seventh principle of the art of *stalking* tells that the *stalker*-teacher – Nagual – never pushes in the first row and always watches from behind the scenes.

The shamans know that the *stalkers*, applying the seven principles of the art of *stalking*, achieve three results.

The three results of *stalking*

The first result of the art of *stalking* is achieved when the *stalker* learns to make fun of himself, never to take himself seriously.

The second result of the art of *stalking* is attained when the *stalker* learn never to be in a hurry and to acquire an unlimited patience.

The third result of the art of *stalking* is attained when the *stalker* learns to have an enormous ability of improvisation.

The ancient shamans *saw* how the Eagle, thru its emanations, gives awareness – awareness B – at the moment of the birth of the living beings, so that it may be enriched thru the life experiences. They also *saw* how the Eagle, still by means of its emanations, after the living beings' death takes back their enriched awareness. Moreover, they *saw* that when it found itself facing the death of shamans who had recapitulated their own existence, in a formal way, it had a moment of hesitation.

From these observations, they came to the conclusion that the Eagle searches for the life experiences and that it had to be satisfied with an imitation of these experiences. They comprehended that only with an exhaustive and perfect *recapitulation* a copy of genuine awareness could have been generated, a surrogate which, given by the Eagle, would have set them free to reach *infinity*.

The second way of proceeding in order to carry out the *recapitulation* is exhaustive and perfect. It consists of gathering in a mnemonic album all the memorable moments – unforgettable moments – of one's existence.

It's a collection of all those events holding a particular meaning in the shaman's existence – man of knowledge – and which, besides testifying his life's circumstances they also reveal his personality.

The shaman's memorable events have "the touch of impersonal", that is they concern every human being, not only him. They are representations of man's nature, stories in which the shaman is not the center of attention and, even if they don't concern him, they involve him all life long.

The shaman carries out the *recapitulation* combining it with the walking – it helps to stir up the memories – and with a specific respiratory technique. Slow inhalations are made, turning almost imperceptibly the head from right to left, and at the same way exhalations are made turning the head from left to right.

The exhaustive *recapitulation*, since it's perfect, allows compressing the proto-energy bubble. This is possible because the man of knowledge's *assemblage point* shifts a little leftwards in the position known as "pitilessness". It's a permanent *change*, a *modification* inside the organic part of the big human band. It has as result the mutation of the former energetic form. The oval-shaped bubble compresses so that it appears gravestone-shaped and green-colored. Furthermore, the breach that is on the bubble – in correspondence of the umbilical zone – shrinks.

The album of memorable events is an exercise in impartiality in order to gather the global whole of one's emotions and fulfillments; it is the instrument for the re-settlement of the emotional and energetic arrangement and for the reuse of one's unused energy in order to face *infinity*.

The collection of the existence's memorable events represents, to the shaman, the required preparation to face "the ultimate journey"... a journey that's possible after the physical death. The organic body, instead of decomposing, turns into pure energy and the inorganic body gets thicker, becoming solid – twice – but inaccessible by the normal perception.

The third way of proceeding in order to carry out the *recapitulation* is fluent and impeccable. It consists of recapitulating, without an apparent order, different episodes of one's life... what shamans call "recapitulation of the pieces of a jigsaw puzzle".

In order to recapitulate in this way "the Master of Ceremonies" must be made emerged on the screen of memory, an event that is remembered with extreme neatness and surprising clearness of details, so that it is relived – one literally sinks in it – and that opens the way of 'reliving' episodes of one's existence.

The shaman carries out the *recapitulation* making "the

mind to be quiet" and evoking the *intent*, that is he breaks the stream of the thoughts for a few moments and lets his *intent* to choose the event to be 'relived'. With this he combines a specific respiratory technique and a way of moving his head – to fan the episode – from side to side.

The shaman makes long and deep inhalations, turning slowly his head from left to right in a 180 degrees arc. After inhaling, he exhales in the same way, turning his head from right to left.

The fluent and impeccable *recapitulation* allows 'recalling' the experience to the mind – to relive totally – and this happens when the *intent* shifts the *assemblage point* in a specific position, allowing the shaman to 'relive' the event.

The fluent *recapitulation*, since it's impeccable, allows compressing the proto-energy bubble. This is possible because the man of knowledge's *assemblage point* shifts a little leftwards, in the position known as "hard pitilessness". It's a permanent *change*, a *modification* inside the organic part of the big human band. It has as result the mutation of the former energetic form. The gravestone-shaped and green-colored bubble compresses so that it appears in the shape of an amber-colored compressed gravestone. Furthermore, the breach that is on the bubble – in correspondence of the umbilical zone – shrinks.

Don Juan revealed me, while I was in the silent perception state, that the man of knowledge had to accomplish three achievements in order to lose completely his conceit – personal importance – and acquire pitilessness (sobriety).

The first achievement – to lose initially conceit – consists of shifting and fixing the *assemblage point* in "pitilessness", whereas the second one – to lose further conceit – consists of shifting and fixing the *assemblage point* in " hard pitilessness". Finally, the third one – to lose completely conceit – consists of achieving the symbolic but definitive death.

After these three achievements the shaman is ready to shift

and fix the *assemblage point* in the high perception state, the precursor of the intense perception state. In this state the mind is still able to remember what has happened even if one lives in an altered state, similar to a dream.

In this state the seer's *assemblage point* shifts leftwards and fixes beyond the central line of the proto-energy bubble. It's a permanent *change*, a *modification* inside the organic part of the big human band that, at first, shows up with the loss of the will of living. This happens because the *assemblage point* fixes in the man's left side.

In the high perception state the shaman – without sense of conceit – can apply the *controlled folly*, a way of being that allows him to behave with people in a particular way. He – unlike common men – is aware that his acts are not important; he knows that exist more or less important actions because facing death it all depends. He's conscious that the men's way of living is folly and so he wields a control on folly – *controlled folly* – of his life. However his acts are true and sincere, even if they are only the acts of an actor.

The shaman, wielding the *controlled folly*, applies the seven principles of the art of *stalking* in a social context. He's able to pretend to be completely immersed – like an actor on the stage – in what he's doing without one would suspect he's faking.

The *controlled folly* is the artistic technique of the art of *stalking*; it allows to be separated from everything yet remaining an integral part of everything, and it's the only bridge between people's folly – the usual human behavior – and the dictates' strictness – control – of the Eagle.

In another session of his teachings don Juan revealed me, while I was in the silent perception state, that the Eagle is the great tyrant, the supreme monarch of the universe. Below it, was the category of tyrants, the Nagual-masters. Then, more below, was the category of small tyrants, the torturers that have the power of life and death on men. At the end, below all the others, was the category of tiny tyrants, those who make life impossible. The latters were divided in different typologies, according to their inclinations.

He explained me that the man of knowledge could lose personal importance using a small tyrant – or a tiny tyrant – and in doing so he had to control, systematically, his behaviour through ten features (control, discipline, detachment, decision, balance, astuteness, patience, kindness, indifference and timing).

He added that seers, now free of personal importance, had acquired the eleventh feature – pitilessness – and using a small tyrant – or a tiny tyrant – they could master *intent* obtaining the connection of all the twelve features.

The shaman must learn the eighth principle – or the absolute first – of the art of *stalking*.

The eighth principle of *stalking*

The eighth principle – or the absolute first – of the art of *stalking* tells that the shaman must *stalk* himself.

To *stalk* oneself means to shake oneself – using one's behavior with astuteness and pitilessness – in order to strengthen one's connection ring which is situated between the reason and the silent knowledge.

To strengthen – sensitize – one's connection ring with the silent knowledge of the Eagle's *intent*, it needs to change continually from the normal perception state to the intense perception state.

The sensitization of the connection ring with the silent knowledge of the *intent* allows the shaman to know without knowing, that is to intuit everything without mistaking. Error can be only in case of involvement of personal feelings that can darken the connection ring.

The eighth principle of *stalking* allows the shaman to apply the first seven principles in the everyday life. He builds a 'building' – theatrical performance – under the direct control of the *intent* and he's the leading actor behind the scenes.

The shaman, to build a *building*, must "wake the intent", that is he must state his intentions, yet without revealing his real aim to his action's recipients.

Several people enter the *building* – common men and warriors – and the theatrical performance is created in order to put the warriors facing the contrast that occurs between the folly of the people and the control of the Eagle. Suddenly the folly of the people gets the upper hand on the warriors but at the end it's overwhelmed by the far-seeing design of the Eagle.

Don Juan revealed me, while I was in the silent perception state, the secret of the First, Second, Third and Fourth Attention.

The First Attention is the world of people how they normally conceive it. Its secret is explained by the fact that the warrior-*stalker* can create, by means of his energy situated in the umbilical zone, an energetic double – *soul* – of himself. This double – *body of intent* – has a will of his own (the copy of the warrior's awareness) independent of the *stalker*.

The Second Attention is a world configured in relation to the direct experience of the shaman. To enter it, it needs to "shrink the tonal" and "make the nagual to appear". It needs to take the *tonal* by surprise (awareness A) making it to lose control for the advantage of the *nagual* (awareness B) which gets the upper hand. In practice, the physical body turns into energy and takes on the temporal physical body – it owns a proto-energy bubble – in the Second Attention. Then the shaman wields the will to return in the First Attention to take on his physical body again.

The Third Attention is a world – sulphureous zone – situated between the parallel lines (the world of the men and the other world are sited on two parallel lines). It is a frontier area looking like a desert zone with sulfur-like yellowish dunes.

The warrior-*stalker* can enter the Third Attention both in

the very hard intense perception state and in the normal perception state.

The *stalker*, in the very hard intense perception state, perceives an immense yellowish fog bank which divides the world into two and goes from the ground to the sky. He's turned eastwards and the other half of the world on his left – north – remains clear, while the half on his right – south – is misted by the fog bank.

The warrior, turning his head, makes the wall to turn in the direction of rotation and when he takes on the magical body – *shabodo* – the wall's rotation stops. The magical body is a duplicate of the body of the *stalker*, a three-dimensional image of temporal energy penetrated by a proto-energy bubble.

The warrior, in the moment when he takes on the *shabodo*, rotates with his magical body – coinciding with the physical body – for 90 degrees rightwards, finding the wall of fog in front of him. Thus he has the chance to cross it and enter the Third Attention. Then he comes back and re-enter the physical body.

The *stalker*, in the normal perception state, uses the humito – little smoke – to enter the Third Attention. He takes on the *shabodo*, faces and overcomes the *guardian* of the sulphureous world and penetrates the Third Attention. Then he comes back and re-enters the physical body.

Furthermore, the *stalker* can enter the sulphureous zone with the *dreaming body*, the space-time physical body penetrated by a proto-energy bubble.

To take on the *dreaming body* it needs to be divided at perception's level – the perception of one's being must be divided between the right and the left side – and to perceive the two hemispheres of the brain as two separate beings.

In practice, one is divided at perceptive level by the double whisper of the two masters – the teacher whispers at the right ear and the benefactor at the left one – which cause a splitting on the upper side of the proto-energy bubble. Then, thru the splitting on the bubble, one is pulled out by the two teachers.

After that a dimensional breach is opened between the First and the Third Attention and one enters the sulphureous world with the *dreaming body*. Finally, one comes back and re-enters the physical body thru the splitting on the bubble.

The Fourth Attention is a world – the other world – that appears as a scenery abundant in vegetation with mountains, hills, rivers and plains.

The warrior-*stalker* can enter the Fourth Attention in the very hard intense perception state or in the normal perception state.

The *stalker*, in the very hard intense perception state, turns eastwards and perceives, on his right, the wall of yellowish fog.

The warrior, in the moment when he takes on the *shabodo*, rotates with his magical body – coinciding with the physical body – for 90 degrees rightwards, finding the fog bank in front of him. He keeps still staring at it and then he directly enters the Fourth Attention. Then he comes back and re-enters the physical body.

The *stalker*, in the normal perception state, uses his will-power – or the little smoke – to enter the Fourth Attention. He sees a monumental door – a breach between the First and the Third Attention – and crosses it with his *shabodo*. After entering the sulphureous zone he sets out on a journey to reach a highland, on which there's the entrance to the other world. He goes across it yelling and enters the Fourth Attention. Then he sets out on the return journey.

The warrior, still in the normal perception state, enters the Fourth Attention thru *sleeping*. In practice, the *sleeper* comes into an inner silence state and slides into sleep with the *intent* to take on the *shabodo* and entering the other world. In the moment when he takes on the *shabodo*, he's turned southwards and rotates with his magical body – coinciding with the physical body – for 90 degrees leftwards, finding the Fourth Attention in front of him. In this way he has the chance to enter the other world. Then he comes back and re-enters the physical body.

The warrior, after losing his *human form*, starts seeing, in the normal perception state, an eye in front of him – dimensional door – which allows him to enter the Fourth Attention. In practice, the shapeless *stalker* closes his eyes, sees the eye and starts *sleeping*. At this point the *sleeper* takes on the *shabodo* and crosses the dimensional door to enter the other world. Then he comes back and re-enters the physical body.

Don Juan explained to me, while I was in the silent perception state, that at the basis of our being there's the perception. It is divided into three parts.

The first part is the Attention of the Tonal, the "first ring of power", that is the ability of the individual to put his perception in the world of everyday life, the known.

The second part is the Attention of the Nagual, the "second ring of power", that is the ability of the man of knowledge to put his perception in unusual worlds, the unknown, the almost untold unknown, the untold unknown.

The third part is the Attention of the Eagle, the "third ring of power", that is the ability of the seer to put his perception in direct contact with the great tyrant, the unknowable.

In the following meetings Don Juan explained to me that the ancient shamans, thanks to the fact that they had recapitulated in an exhaustive and perfect way, they could attain, a few hours after their physical death, the physicized *shabodo* with the consequent disintegration – transformation into pure energy – of the organism. Whereas the modern shamans carry out "the final passage" when they are still alive, since the *passage* is a "unifying factor".

He told me that the modern shamans, thanks to the fact that they recapitulate in a fluent and impeccable way, they achieve the symbolic but definitive death. This allows them, after, to carry out the *finale passage*.

He informed me that they all – he and his follower shamans – took on, in the high perception state, the physicized *shabodo*. In an a-temporal fraction their physical body became not-

fragmentary energy and their magical body got thicker. Then they opened the slit wide – *cosmic vagina* – between the First and the Fourth Attention and slipped away thru it.

Finally he revealed me that an external observer, *seeing them* in the moment when they were taking on their inorganic bodies, would have been under the impression that the proto-energy bubbles of their physical bodies were lighting up with brightness. But what the observer *sees* is the lit bubble of the inorganic body.

When I started the drawing up of this book some ancient shamans, who live in the Fourth Attention, came to me to reveal me the way of *stalking together*.

"We are the ancient shamans lived thousands years ago, at the beginning of human civilization. We are an indefinite number. We follow the Eagle's designs and every now and then, when the Eagle asks us to, we intervene on human beings so that they make experiences.

"Unlike common men the shamans have the illusion to have more power, actually they are born to carry out in a more conscious way the dictates of the *intent*, even after the biological life, but nobody knows why! For exchange, the *intent* lets decide what to do of one's life.

"They defined us as the *silent ones*, 'those who silently pass', since when we act we don't make ourselves heard".

4

The practice of *dreaming*

The sorcerers of the ancient times developed the most obscure of the magic arts and named it the practice of *dreaming*, which is essentially based on the dreams' control. It produces a movement leftwards of the *dreamer*'s *assemblage point* and this allows activating some internal filaments, usually never used, in the proto-energy bubble, widening awareness and perception.

The ancient sorcerers put a series of procedures right in order to wield a systematic control – to act deliberately – on their dreams' situations and to perceive inorganic worlds. To them, *dreaming* represented a practical way of manipulating common dreams, till usual standards of differentiation between dream and reality were no more valid.

The sorcerers of the ancient times learned *dreaming* while they were in the normal perception state – like shamans of modern times learn it – because *dreaming* is very dangerous.

To start oneself in *dreaming*, something inactive inside oneself must be awakened, that is that part of the residual awareness which is even kept sleeping. This is the Attention of the Dream.

The modern shamans know – like ancient sorcerers did – that perseverance is the active element which allows to develop the *dreaming*, that is to wield a systematic control on one's dreams and, in the meantime, to strengthen one's Attention of the Dream.

The seers consider the *dreaming* as an extremely refined practice which allows shifting the *assemblage point* from its usual position in order to intensify perception. While one is dreaming, the *assemblage point* shifts slowly in a natural way and the shamans use the *dream* to control – to fix – this movement. Deeper the movement – fixing – of the *assemblage point* more concrete is the dream. It follows that to interfere in dreams means to interfere in the natural movement of the *assemblage point*.

Dreaming draws the attention of alien entities – entities that own temporal bodies absorbed by alien proto-energy – and forces them into appearing in the sorcerer's dreams. But to attain an optimal result, the sorcerer must add to the *dreaming* the *intent* to want to meet them in the *dream*.

In dreamland exists a threshold, a passage that allows the alien entities to enter man's world of dreams and the *dreamers*, who express the *intent* to follow them, to enter the twelve worlds – six related to the element of water and six associated to the element of fire – of Attention Zero. Each world owns a *guardian* who shows up to the *dreamer* as an entity or as a voice – the voice of the *dream*'s *emissary* – which offers to help him.

The six worlds – related to the water element – are structurally similar and differ only in the form of the mobile inorganic beings. I confine myself, only, to describing the first three ones because the more we penetrate the worlds the more the power of the entities that dwell there increases, generating dangerous interferences in the human consciousness. Moreover, I can't describe the other six worlds – related to the fire element – because my benefactor, the death opponent, fell a prey to *aqueous* alien entities, and he knows nothing about *igneous* alien entities and their worlds.

The first world – related to the water element – is a porous and cavernous world with a rough and fibrous structure. On the inside several geometrical tunnels go in all directions. The tunnels are immobile inorganic beings that can project themselves, while the mobile inorganic beings' forms are of three kinds: round, bell-shaped and candle-flame-shaped (scouts). This world's *guardian* is a bell-shaped inorganic being and the scouts own a slightly-fizzing energy.

The second world – related to the water element – is structurally similar to the first one and differs only in the form of the mobile inorganic beings which are of two kinds: mobile shades (scouts) and a second kind which is revealed only to those *dreamers* who decide to remain in this world, expressing the *intent* in a loud voice. The *guardian* – mobile shade – of this world is an inorganic being who appears as a gland-like protuberance and the scouts own an energy that looks like it's on the point of burning.

The third world – associated to the water element – is structurally similar to the first one and differs only in the form of the mobile inorganic beings which is of one kind: cylindrical (scouts). The *guardian* of this world is a cylinder-shaped inorganic being and the scouts own an energy laden with hatred.

The shamans bind the practice of *dreaming* to three essential conditions: the foundation of the *dreaming*, to start *dreaming* and to organize the *dreaming*.

The foundation of *dreaming* consists of intending – to want without wishing – to be a *dreamer*, even if one is not yet. It needs to have the will – silent determination – to become a *dreamer* and the conviction to be one.

In order to start *dreaming* it needs to express the *intent*, shortly before falling asleep, to become conscious – during the sleep – to be dreaming.

To organize the *dreaming* a systematic control must be wielded on one's dreams. It needs to prevent one's dream from transforming into another one until one decides to change it.

All this involves a struggle of the mind with itself.

There are eight doors, experimented as obstacles – which the *dreamers* must enter in order to achieve perfection in the practice of *dreaming*. They call them the eight gates of *dreaming*.

The first gate of *dreaming*

To intend the first gate of *dreaming* means to express the *intent* to manage to bear the sight of anything one is looking at in his dream.

To reach the first gate of *dreaming* means to carry out one's *intent* in the dream.

In practice, in order to carry out one's *intent* in the dream, one must focus the look on any component of the dream and then shift it on other elements. Thus one's attention is focused on the dream's components – *dreaming vigilance* – and the images become more substantial, and this prevents the dream from becoming evanescent. In this way one wields his Attention of the Dream.

To win the first gate of *dreaming* means to manage to locate and isolate an alien entity, and the *dreamers* usually do it after having lost their *human form*.

The loss of the *human form* allows to become a shapeless *dreamer* who gives up his attachment to things and people, and thus in the body appears a certain tension and a loss of energy. At this point the alien proto-energy penetrates in the *dreamer*'s body thru the world of dreams and causes a situation where calmness, balance and emotional solidness are not favored.

Behind the elements present in the dreams can hide alien entities, related to the element of the water or of the fire, which must be located and isolated. In practice, one's Attention of the Dream discovers the alien entity behind the component of a dream and focuses on it with extreme intensity, forcing it into interacting with awareness. Thus the global dream collapses leaving only the entity which conveys to the brain a discharge similar to electrical current and this allows the formation of the inner *shabodo* which owns the alien proto-energy bubble. The so produced *shabodo* results to be of the same nature of the alien entity and thus a certain dependence establishes towards it. In fact, when one springs out of a dream he finds himself in his inner *shabodo* in an obscure not-dream dimension. Then one rises up turning whirls around, pulled by the entity, unable to control one's inner *shabodo*.

The second gate of *dreaming*

To reach the second gate of *dreaming* means to wake up from a dream in another dream.

There are three ways to wake up from a dream in another dream. The first way involves that, during the first dream, one dreams to make a second dream and dreams to wake up from it, finding himself in the latter. The second way implies that, while one dreams, it needs to use an element of the dream in order to wake up in another dream, from the image of the dream to the dream of the image. The third way consists of expressing the *intent* to want to move from a dream to another and to do this one must turn the head from right to left and vice versa, focusing the look only on the furthermost points of one's rotation. In this way the *intent* is attracted with the eyes and moves the *assemblage point*, producing another dream.

To win the second gate of *dreaming* means to strengthen one's Attention of the Dream so that to experiment the total Attention of the Dream.

To strengthen one's Attention of the Dream means to focus it on the objects of the dreams, so that to see them substantial. So the control on one's dreams is attained and one accomplishes the total Attention of the Dream, which occurs when the *assemblage point* fixes in a specific position. In practice, the technique consists of falling asleep in a particular position of the physical body (on the right side, on the left side, on one's back or prone) and thus to wake up in that position in a concrete *dream*.

To cross the second gate of *dreaming* means to locate and follow the alien entities in their worlds (inner Attention Zero).

At this point there are two ways of proceeding, according to the ancient sorcerers and according to the modern shamans.

The ancient sorcerers ruled over a vast geographic area – Mexico – for five thousand years, from eight thousand to three thousand years ago. And their obscure practices drove them to be bound to the alien entities, in order to become intermediaries between the men's world and the entities' one. At their physical death they, inexorably, fell a prey to the alien entities. To this category of sorcerers belongs the death opponent who came to me to teach me the secret teachings of Nagualism.

The death opponent remained entrapped in the Kingdom of Attention Zero for about six thousand years. Then he managed, using a skillful stratagem, to take on a woman's aspect and so he had, automatically, been expelled from that Kingdom that does not accept the feminine element. The ancient sorcerer lavishes power gifts to the Naguals in exchange for energy. He inserts his *aqueous shabodo*'s rod in the split – in correspondence of the navel – of the Nagual's proto-energy bubble. Then he enlarges it and receives a strong discharge of alien proto-energy that he accumulates inside him.

The modern shamans, instead, choose to free themselves from the alien entities and to do this they make contact with the first entity they have located and isolated. They control it by means of their will, feeling detachment. After that, since they spring out of a dream, they find themselves with their inner *shabodo*, in an obscure not-dream dimension. Then they express the will to control their inner *shabodo* and, moving, they find that the only way to do it is to slide or to fly high.

The third gate of *dreaming*

To reach the third gate of *dreaming* means to look oneself asleep.

In order to look oneself asleep it needs to exteriorize with one of the two *shabodos* out of the physical body and remain there, for a few moments, to watch the sleeping body. Then the *shabodo* is moved by means of the mind. Once the *shabodo* is formed, related to one of the two elements, one is also able to form the other one.

To win the third gate of *dreaming* means to *see* the alien proto-energy with the inner *shabodo* and the proto-energy with the exteriorized *shabodo*.

In order to *see* with the inner *shabodo* the elements of the dreams it needs to utter the *intent* to do it and after that the silent volition will be sufficient. To the *dreamer* it will happen to *see* among the various phantasm images (images that don't produce any kind of energy) the elements that generate alien proto-energy (obscure and sizzling proto-energy).

In order to *see* with the exteriorized *shabodo* it needs to express the *intent* with one's silent volition. To the *dreamer* it will happen to *see* the proto-energy in everyday world (clear and vibrating proto-energy).

The fourth gate of *dreaming*

To reach the fourth gate of *dreaming* means to carry out the technique of the twin positions.

There are four variations of the exercise to start *dreaming*: to put the physical body on the right side, on the left side, on one's back or prone. For example, one can fall asleep on the right side with the knees a little bent and then wake up in that position in a concrete *dream*, carrying out the total Attention of the Dream. Soon after one falls asleep for the second time in the same position and wakes up in an even more concrete *dream*. Then, to get back in a wakefulness state, one goes from the second *dream* to the first one and from the latter to wakefulness. Thus the two positions got during the *dreams* form an unit – the twin positions of *dreaming* – and the deep Attention of the Dream is carried out, and it occurs when the *assemblage point* fixes deeply in a specific position.

To win the fourth gate of *dreaming* means to travel to places that exist only in the *intent dream* of those who won this gate.

The mystery of *intent* in the total Attention of the Dream for the twin positions consists of being drawn, with the inner *shabodo*, into the *intent dream* of whom carried it out and then of being brought in his second *dream*.

The fifth gate of *dreaming*

To reach the fifth gate of *dreaming* means to wake up in the most concrete *dream* one can imagine.

In practice, to wake up in the most concrete *dream*, one must express the *intent*, shortly before falling asleep, to wake up in an extremely concrete *dream*. The accomplishment of this *dream* allows to carry out the intensified Attention of the Dream that occurs when the *assemblage point* fixes intensely in a specific position.

To win the fifth gate of *dreaming* means to carry out the intensified Attention of the Dream and from it to wake up in the First inner Attention with the inner spatial physical body.

The sixth gate of *dreaming*

To reach the sixth gate of *dreaming* means to experiment the Second inner Attention.

In order to experiment the Second inner Attention one must

stare at an object of the dream, so intensely to find oneself in the Second inner Attention with the inner temporal physical body.

To win the sixth gate of *dreaming* means to wake up in the Second Attention's subjective ocean with the temporal physical body.

To wake up in the Second Attention allows to attain the total perception of the experimented world and the total cohesion of the taken body.

To cross the sixth gate of *dreaming* means to get intentionally alien proto-energy from the Attention Zero, a very mysterious maneuver consisting of *stalking the stalkers*.

In practice, to *stalk the stalkers*, awareness B is used to move, by means of the alien proto-energy, to the Second Attention. The temporal physical body is wrapped up by this proto-energy and awareness B is clouded. Therefore, it needs to fight with all one's strength to regain lucidity, in order to get back to the First Attention.

To consolidate the sixth gate of *dreaming* means to choose to live in the Second Attention forever.

In practice, to live forever in the Second Attention, specific steps are to be done. The first step consists of staring at an object and visualizing it with one's eyes closed. The second one consists of projecting one's *intent* into the dream that is to *dream* the object – Attention of the Dream – and to embody it totally – total Attention of the Dream – in order to win the first stage towards total perception. The third step consists of the collective visualization – in group – of a site, to *dream* it and to embody it totally to win the second stage towards total perception. The fourth step is to reproduce the Second Attention's site, that is to move in group to an objective island of the Second Attention's immense subjective ocean. In this way one acquires uniformity and cohesion beyond the First Attention, and this action is defined by the ancient sorcerers as "the perception stalking", the third and last stage towards the achievement of total perception.

The seventh gate of *dreaming*

To reach the seventh gate of *dreaming* means to divide one's being's perception between the right and the left side.

To divide one's being's perception it needs to break its unity, perceiving the two hemispheres of the brain as two separate beings. In practice, in a dreaming state, one is divided at perceptive level by a teacher who, with his *shabodo*, cause a splitting on the upper side of the proto-energy bubble.

To win the seventh gate of *dreaming* means to experiment the *dreaming body* – space-time physical body – in the First Attention.

To experiment in a dreaming state the space-time physical body one must find his hands in the dream and stare intensively at them, so that to come out from the skull with one's *dreaming body*.

To cross the seventh gate of *dreaming* means to open a dimensional breach between the First and the Third Attention and enter in the sulphureous zone (Third Attention) with the space-time physical body.

To consolidate the seventh gate of *dreaming* means to choose to live in the Third Attention forever.

In practice, in order to live forever in the Third Attention, one opens the dimensional breach between the First and the Third Attention and enters in group in the sulphureous zone. This action is defined by the ancient sorcerers as "the dream of perception".

The eighth gate of *dreaming*

To reach the eighth gate of *dreaming* means to accomplish the procedure of *dreaming together*.

In practice, to accomplish the procedure of *dreaming*

together, the two *dreamers* must start a *dream* from two different locations. The first who starts *dreaming* penetrates in the *dream* of the other one and 'seize' him, that is he grabs his arm. Thus the first *dreamer* shares the *dream* of the second one.

To win the eighth gate of *dreaming* means to accomplish the procedure of *sleeping together*.

In practice, to accomplish the procedure of *sleeping together*, the *sleepers* enter into a state of total inner silence and slide into sleep with the *intent* to wake up in the Third Attention with the *shabodo*.

There are two ways of proceeding to cross the eighth gate of *dreaming*, according to the ancient sorcerers and according to the modern shamans.

The ancient sorcerers gave the disciples the chance to cross the eighth gate of *dreaming* by recruiting the alien beings – *aqueous* or *igneous* – who took the disciples into the Attention Zero. In practice, in an awake or asleep state, two alien entities stimulated, one from a side and one from the other, two specific points – in correspondence of the right hip and left hip zone – on the disciple's proto-energy bubble who found himself with the temporal physical body – *aqueous shabodo* or *igneous shabodo* – in the Attention Zero. Then he went back to the First Attention with the power to be the go-between of the two Attentions.

The modern shamans, instead, give their disciples the chance to cross the eighth gate of *dreaming* by making them to get intentionally alien proto-energy from the Attention Zero, a very mysterious maneuver consisting of *stalking the dreamers* (the last *stalking*). In practice, the procedure of *sleeping together* is accomplished and awareness B is used in order to shift and fix the *assemblage point* to enter, by means of the alien proto-energy, the Third Attention with the phyisicized *shabodo*. Then one expresses the *intent* to enter the Fourth Attention until he owns the alien proto-energy.

There are two ways of proceeding to consolidate the eighth gate of *dreaming*, according to the ancient sorcerers and according to the modern shamans.

The ancient sorcerers consolidated the eighth gate of *dreaming* by deciding to remain forever in the Attention Zero.

The modern shamans, instead, consolidate the eighth gate of *dreaming* by deciding to stay in the Fourth Attention forever.

In the context of don Juan's secret knowledge the fixing of the Attention of the Dream has two aspects.

The first aspect is when the shamans use the *dreaming* to concentrate – fixing – the Attention of the Dream on things that are not of this world, like the journey in unknown. When the shamans learn to concentrate on the bright side of the Attention of the Dream, nothing can hinder them. They become the *dreamers of infinity*.

The second aspect is when the shamans use the *dreaming* to concentrate – fixing – the Attention of the Dream on things of this world, like the material power. When the shamans learn to concentrate on the dark side of the Attention of the Dream, nothing can hinder them. They become the *dreamers of the abyss*.

The keys of power

The magic formulae of *dreaming* for *stalking* and of *stalking* for *dreaming* are the keys of power.

Dreaming for stalking

The shaman chooses, in an awake state, a topic for *dreaming*.

The shaman visualizes mentally the topic – in the form of thought or image – and goes into the inner silence state. Then, during the night, he *dreams* it, so that he can reproduce it in the course of the day.

Stalking for dreaming

The shaman chooses, in an *oneiric* state, an act for *waking up*.

The shaman does a particular act – in the form of positions or movements – in the *dream*, towards another person. Then, during the day, he *wakes him up*, reproducing positions and movements (magic steps). Thus the act is replicated in the *dream* of the *dreamed* person.

5

The mastery of *intent*

The shamans of ancient times *saw*, thanks to the use of psychotropic plants, the impersonal energy coming from the Eagle's emanations – the dark-bright sea of *infinity* – and named it "strength-will", the active aspect of *infinity*. Furthermore, they realized that the strength-will was directly responsible of human beings' perception – it lights up a little part of filaments inside the proto-energy bubble – and indirectly of the dislocation of their *assemblage points*.

The ancient shamans *saw*, still thanks to the use of the psychotropic plants, how the strength-will moved the *assemblage point* and how the latter, shifting, regulated man's perception. Then they decided to manipulate this kind of energy – impersonal power – and to do this they developed the most powerful of magic arts, the mastery of *intent*.

The mastery of *intent* is essentially based on the control of the *assemblage point* that allows *seeing* the proto-energy. It produces a movement leftwards of the seer's *assemblage point* and this allows activating some internal filaments, usually never used, in the proto-energy bubble, widening awareness and perception.

When don Juan came to me – with his inorganic body – he

revealed to me, while I was in the silent perception state, that there has been a time, about eight thousand years ago, in which two factions of seers arose: the ancient shamans of the *stalkers*' line and the ancient sorcerers of the *dreamers*' line.

He told me that the two factions were constantly in combat and that the first one was leaded by the four-forked Naguals, while the second one was headed by the three-forked Naguals.

He told me that later, about three thousand years ago, a new cycle of seers of the *stalkers*' line arose, and that the cycle of the seers of the *dreamers*' line ended, without any chance for a new beginning.

Don Juan told me that he belonged to a twenty-seven-generations dynasty of shamans and that, around the end of the sixteenth century, during the Spanish conquest, each Nagual isolated with his followers, giving birth to individual stocks. His one, as an individual stock, was constituted by fifteen men Naguals, sixteen women Naguals and one hundred forty-four shamans. Some of these Naguals had as followers eight, or twelve, or sixteen shamans.

He explained to me that his lineage, at the beginning of the eighteenth century, passed thru a drastic change when the death opponent came on the scene, an ancient sorcerer – who lived about six thousand years ago – of the *dreamers*' line. This sorcerer contacted the Nagual Sebastian and, in exchange for energy, he gave him some power gifts. Furthermore, he taught him the ancient practices of *dreaming* even if the Nagual did not belong to the *dreamers*' line. The influence was such that Sebastian and the six Naguals who succeeded to him were intrinsically different from the eight who had preceded them.

He told me that the Naguals, belonging to the *stalkers*' line, have a natural inclination for *stalking* or for *dreaming* and he revealed me the last seven Naguals' natural inclination: Sebastian-*dreamer*, Santisteban-*stalker*, Lujan-*dreamer*, Rosendo-*stalker*, Elias-*dreamer*, Julian-*stalker*, Juan-*dreamer*.

Don Juan informed me that his lineage could have continued only if he had met a four-forked Nagual inclined to *stalking.* Instead his stock ended with Castaneda's appearance, a three-forked Nagual of the *dreamers*' line who, like all the sorcerers, was inclined to *dreaming*. But, thru Castaneda, he could spread in the world his knowledge and thus close his lineage with a "golden key".

He told me that his cycle of seers – that of the *stalkers*' line – had ended and that a new cycle of seers was coming up, that of the *artists*' line with a natural inclination for *power*, that natural inclination that allows interacting with the Eagle.

He revealed to me that I was the first Nagual of a new stock of sorcerers, more powerful, more pitiless… and this was due to the fact that my bubble had a special proto-energetic configuration that the seers *saw* as a three-four-compartmented sphere, since one of the sections-dividing lines was not well defined.

Don Juan reminded me that the energetically predominant individual inside a group of shamans was called Nagual, a person – man or woman – who, thanks to his (her) extraordinary energetic capability, was responsible for his (her) group's destiny, the ideal guide – natural chief – in warriors' life.

He told me that the Naguals, in their capacity as go-betweens, canalized the learning directly from the silent knowledge of the Eagle's *intent* and conveyed it to their mates. Furthermore, they had the responsibility to give their disciples what the shamans called "the least possibility", that is the awareness-perception of their link – connection ring – with the silent knowledge of the *intent of infinity*.

He told me that the Nagual man was a teacher endowed with resistance and firmness who brought sobriety, while the Nagual woman brought innovation. In his function of chief he had to behave in the most efficient and impeccable way, since he could not plan rationally the course of his actions… course that was decided by the Eagle's *intent*.

Don Juan explained to me that the affiliation to the world of magic implied to have faith in the Nagual, that is to learn to trust completely the Nagual and to accept him without reservations. If there was no faith in the Nagual there was no chance to empty one's life of the litter and thus to be free.

Finally, he revealed to me the secret part of the three-forked Nagual's rule, the one concerning me.

Three-four-forked Nagual's rule

The Eagle gives the three-four-forked Nagual (it appears as a pair, male and female), as companions, three *dreamer-stalker* she-warriors, three *dreamer-stalker* warriors and a messenger.

Furthermore, it gives the task to find three other *dreamer-stalker* she-warriors, three *dreamer-stalker* warriors and a messenger.

Dreamer-stalker women are named the four directions, the four winds, the four different female personalities existing in human race.

The first one is the north, the second one is the west, the third one is the east and the fourth one is the south. The three-four-forked Nagual woman represents the south.

Dreamer-stalker men represent the four directions, the four kinds of male activity and temperament.

The first one is the north, the second one is the east, the third one is the west and the fourth one is the south.

So people under a three-four-forked Nagual's guidance are in the number of fourteen: six she-warriors, six warriors and two messengers. With the Nagual man and the Nagual woman they are sixteen in all.

The fundamental cores

In Nagualism there are twenty-one fundamental cores – *intent* cores – which are the concluding subject of the shamanic teaching. They are "shades of perception", levels of our awareness of the Eagle's *intent*.

The twenty-one *intent* cores – abstract cores – are twenty-one recurrent designs, twenty-one *buildings* – complete chains of events – which appear each time the *intent of infinity* shows something important and which constitute the plan, that is the big *building of intent*, *intent*'s silent knowledge.

The big *building of intent* is revealed by means of the shamanic stories and it's of use to know directly the *intent*, without any intervention by the language. This can happen only by cleaning one's connection ring to the silent knowledge of the Eagle's *intent*, and this allows strengthening the relationship with the Eagle itself.

There are hundreds of shamanic stories which are structured upon the fundamental cores, and the reconsideration – systematic analysis – of the acts of the shamans of the past allows to set a "point of reference", providing a chance to re-exam the plan, the twenty-one *intent* cores, the twenty-one *not-doings*.

Don Juan presented to me, while I was in a silent perception state, three groups of seven abstract cores each, at an increasing level of complexity.

The first group comprises the following fundamental cores: the manifestations of *intent*, the touch of *intent*, the stratagem of *intent*, the slope of *intent*, the demands of *intent*, the maneuverability of *intent*, the decision of *intent*.

The manifestations of *intent*

The manifestations of *intent* are given by gestures which show as signals, signs and omens. At the level of the apprentice appear the signals, the world's consents. At the level of the shaman appear the signal, the signs and the omens. Signs are indications, while omens are significant events.

The first shamanic story concerning the *intent*'s manifestations is the report of the relationship between the *intent* and the shaman. About how the *intent* creates a *building* in a second – complete chain of events – in front of the shaman and invites him to enter it with some gestures – signs or omens – which will allow him not to get lost once inside, and on how the *intent* throws a bait for the possible disciple.

The touch of *intent*

The touch of *intent* occurs when the *intent* "knocks at the door" of a man and claims him as a future disciple.

The second shamanic story concerning the touch of *intent* is the report of the relationship between the *intent* and the future disciple. About how the *intent* creates a *building* in a second – complete chain of events – in front of the future disciple and compels him to enter it.

The stratagem of *intent*

The stratagem of *intent* is applied when *intent* uses astuteness and pitilessness in order to shake the future apprentice's connection ring, that is when it cleans up his connection ring to the silent knowledge of the Eagle's *intent*.

The third shamanic story concerning the stratagem of *intent* is the report of how the shaman sets the future apprentice a trap to take him in the magical world. About how the shaman resorts to a subterfuge, using astuteness and pitilessness, to deceive and fool the future disciple, that is to give to his connection ring a jerk with the silent knowledge of the *intent of infinity*.

The slope of *intent*

The slope of *intent* is a "revealing act" occurring when

intent 'drops' on the apprentice and shows itself to him.

The fourth shamanic story concerning the slope of *intent* is the report of how *intent* enables the disciple to reach and cross the *threshold* of unknown. About how *intent* shifts the apprentice's *assemblage point* and lets him to perceive unknown, sealing in this way the everlasting faithfulness of the disciple to *intent*.

The demands of *intent*

The demands of *intent* concern specific positions that *intent* makes the *assemblage point* to assume on the proto-energy bubble of the man of knowledge and the need of the shaman to break the mirror of the reflection of himself.

The fifth shamanic story concerning the demands of *intent* is the report of how *intent* interacts with the shaman. About how *intent* shifts the *assemblage point* of the man of knowledge in specific positions – pitilessness and hard pitilessness – in which pity disappears and oneself reflection is reduced, and on how *intent* demands the shaman to break the mirror of the image of himself by means of his symbolic but definitive death.

The maneuverability of *intent*

The maneuverability of *intent* concerns specific positions that the seer, by means of his *unbending intent*, makes his *assemblage point* to assume on the proto-energy bubble.

The sixth shamanic story concerning the maneuverability of *intent* is the report of how the seer, by means of his *unbending intent*, shifts his *assemblage point*, manipulating his connection ring with *intent*'s silent knowledge. About how the seer shifts his *assemblage point* in certain positions – silent knowledge and divided perception – and experiments the state of "silent knowledge" (knowledge with no words, without language's involvement) and the "double perception" (to perceive two places at the same time, one with the *shabodo*, the other with the physical body).

The decision of *intent*

The decision of *intent* appears when *intent* decides on the direction the shaman must take in his life.

The seventh shamanic story concerning the decision of *intent* is the report of how the shamans behave when the world collapses on them. About how the shamans, facing terrible situations involving them, do their best and then – with no remorse or regrets – relax, letting the *intent* to decide on the result.

Don Juan, after presenting me the first group of seven abstract cores, explained me the relationship shamans have with *intent*.

He told me that inner power – *intent* – of the man of knowledge shows up thru the slit of the power's three points: *intent* (strength-will), *strength* and *will*. And that the split is a slot on the proto-energy bubble of the man situated in the umbilical zone.

He had me know that the man of knowledge has an opening on the bubble that widens – breach – when he becomes approachable to *power*, and in this way his inner power emerges. At first it can be felt as an itch and a heat in the umbilical region, then it becomes a pain and a sick feeling. Finally, when the breach on his bubble shrinks, it becomes an energy that radiates from the umbilical zone after a moment of deep inner silence. It's just this silence – a still more silent moment than that in which the inner dialog is broken – that makes *intent* to arise.

Don Juan told me that the seer moves his *assemblage point* with *intent* and, still with *intent*, he fixes it. And that there are two ways of proceeding to attain this. In the first way the seer is able to transform his moods into *intent* and thus to move and fix his *assemblage point*, while in the second way he's able to evoke the impersonal power in order to experiment a certain state of being.

He explained to me that, in the first way, the seer expresses the intention – he gives himself an order to manipulate sensations – and gets into a specific mood – like euphoria, indisposition, anger, pain, fear – to achieve his own *assemblage point*'s shifting. While, in the second way, the seer attracts with his look and his eyes' sparkling – the eyes are directly connected to the impersonal power – the Eagle's *intent* and expresses a specific intention. Then he enters the inner silence – interruption of the inner dialog – and the *intent of infinity* moves and fixes his *assemblage point* in the specific position that evokes that particular state of being.

Don Juan revealed to me how to accumulate impersonal power to transform it in personal power and thus to develop the third ring of power, the connection ring to learning.

He told me that the impersonal energy accumulated by the man of knowledge becomes personalized energy at his service and that, in order to attain this, the shaman must let his body 'not to do'… not to do what one knows to do. Thus he develops the third ring of power, the connection ring to the silent knowledge of the Eagle's *intent*.

He explained to me that silent knowledge – learning – of the *intent of infinity* is indirectly connected to reason thru intuition and what is called "intuition" is nothing but the activation of the connection – connection ring – to learning. And that, to manipulate one's connection ring to the silent knowledge of the Eagle's *intent*, one must achieve "a certain level of ability", that is one must achieve the pure comprehension… intuition.

Don Juan revealed to me that the seer, after mastering the movement of his *assemblage point*, must get in relation with the Eagle's *intent* in order to carry out his intentions.

He told me that the impersonal power listens only to the seer who talks to it with his 'heart' and with 'gestures'. To speak with one's *heart* means to reveal one's best and to offer it silently to the *power*, while to speak with *gestures* are acts of pure impulse, generosity and shrewdness. In order to address with one's *heart* to the *power*, one must open to feel and offer it, thru the suspension of one's perceptive flow of time, to the *power*. Only in this way the direct connection to the silent knowledge of the *intent of infinity* can occur.

He informed me that the direct connection to the silent knowledge of the Eagle's *intent* works in two ways: to receive information and to send it.

He told that, to receive information, learning – the silent knowledge of the Eagle's *intent* – transmits knowledge directly to feeling – to know something without any doubt – and this occurs thanks to the fact that feeling is situated in the cardiac center that, however, in the modern man is almost quite closed. To open the cardiac center means to open oneself to feeling. While, to send information, feeling transmits knowledge directly to learning and the Eagle's *intent* produces the wanted event. This occurs thanks to the fact that the mind – reason – abstains from formulating consciously the thought and feeling – it contains in essence the wish one wants to see carried out – connects to learning without the mind's addressing the event one wants to see carried out.

Then he presented me the second group of seven fundamental cores: the aspect of *intent*, the influence of *intent*, to *see* the *intent*, the effect of *intent*, the perception of *intent*, the whisper of *intent*, the power of *intent*.

The aspect of *intent*

The aspect of *intent* occurs when the warrior's *assemblage point* shifts into the intense perception state, lighting some unused filaments which memorize information and experiences.

The eighth shamanic story concerning the aspect of *intent* is the report of how the shaman shifts the disciple's *assemblage point* making him live experiences with more intensity – creating him some "island of perception" completely detached among them and from the normal perception state – and about how the warrior, in order to remember, takes his *assemblage point* back to the precise position in which it was when that specific experience occurred.

The influence of *intent*

The influence of *intent* occurs when the seer gets in relation with the Eagle's *intent*, in order to carry out his intentions. And when *intent* expresses thru the Nagual, to make a change in the disciples' level of perception.

The ninth shamanic story concerning the influence of *intent* is the report of how the seer addresses to *intent* with his *heart* – opening to feeling – and with his gestures – acts of pure impulse, generosity, of shrewdness – to carry out his intentions. About how the Nagual lets the *intent* to express thru him so that his disciples may experiment the change from normal perception to the intense one.

To *see* the *intent*

To *see* the *intent* is accomplished when the seer's *assemblage point* shifts and the Eagle's emanations are perceived.

The tenth shamanic story concerning to *see* the *intent* is the report of how the seer *stops the world* and an extraordinary perception shows up in him, to *see*.

The effect of *intent*

The effect of *intent* occurs when *intent*, by means of the teacher, "shrinks the tonal" of the warrior to "make the nagual emerge".

The eleventh shamanic story concerning the effect of *intent* is the report of how *intent*, by means of the teacher, makes the warrior's nagual emerge, making him take on the temporal physical body of the Second Attention.

The perception of *intent*

The perception of *intent* occurs when the warrior breaks the barrier of perception.

The twelfth shamanic story concerning the perception of *intent* is the report of how the warrior breaks the barrier of perception – to perceive the wall of fog and stop its rotation – and takes on the *shabodo* that allows him to enter the Third Attention.

The whisper of *intent*

The whisper of *intent* takes place when the warrior is divided at perception level.

The thirteenth shamanic story concerning the whisper of *intent* is the report of how *intent*, by means of two teachers, divides the perception of the warrior – it causes a splitting on the upper side of the bubble – and makes him take on the *dreaming body* that allows him to enter the Third Attention.

The power of *intent*

The power of *intent* arises when the warrior uses the inner silence to *sleep* and to 'travel'.

The fourteenth shamanic story concerning the power of *intent* is the report of how the warrior goes into the inner silence – sliding into sleep – with the *intent* to take on the *shabodo* to enter the Fourth Attention.

Don Juan, after presenting me the second group of seven abstract cores, explained me that one can *see* the proto-energy thru the refined use of sleep and thru a rigorous and systematic application of the *not-doing*.

He told me that the modern shamans interrupt – *breakpoint* – their old existence's continuity thru the symbolic but definitive death. Only in this way they can intelligently use their new continuity, letting the inner silence to work and to become an active part of their being. This is the ability of the *sleeper* that allows him to guide Eagle's *intent*... to become a *sleeper*-seer.

He had me know that the seers, to *see* the Eagle's emanations and the human beings' proto-energy bubbles, learn to *sleep* – the best way to shift the *assemblage point* – while they are in a normal perception state and that, in order to share the same kind of *vision*, accomplish the procedure of *seeing together*.

Then he explained me how to sink into sleep and apply the *not-doing*.

One goes into a state of perfect calm and to do this he keeps his eyes fixed, without focusing on anything, towards a point just above the horizon line, to heighten the peripheral vision. Then the inner dialog is suspended, the "*not-doing* of talking to oneself", and the inner silence is experimented. In this way one enters a very particular state of sleep in which one is awake and yet asleep, the body is asleep and cannot move but the mind is awake. In this state the ordinary perception collapses – *stopping the world* – and an extraordinary perception shows up, to *see*.

Furthermore, Don Juan revealed to me the main positions of the *assemblage point* in the left side of the man's bubble.

Assemblage point's positions in the left side

In the left side of the bubble there is the position in which one goes into the high perception state, an altered state similar to the dream.

Continuing leftwards there is the position in which one goes into the intense perception state, a state in which information is intensely stored.

Proceeding leftwards there is the position in which, in a normal perception state or in an intense hard perception state, entities are seen in their physical form.

Going on leftwards there is the position in which, in a normal perception state or in an intense harder perception state, the entities are seen as proto-energy bubbles.

Continuing leftwards there is the position in which, in an intense still harder perception state, the *shabodo* is experimented – in relation to the Fourth Attention – in the First Attention.

Proceeding leftwards there is the position in which, in a normal perception state or in an intense highly hard perception state, one enters the Third Attention with his *dreaming body*.

Going on leftwards there is the position in which, in a normal perception state or in an intense deeply hard perception state, the Attention Zero is entered with the *shabodos*.

Continuing leftwards there is the position in which, in a normal perception state or in an intense extremely hard perception state, one enters the Fourth Attention with his *shabodo*.

Finally, proceeding leftwards there is the position in which, in a normal perception state or in an intense very hard perception state, one enters the Second Attention with his temporal body.

Then Don Juan presented to me the third group of seven

fundamental cores: the action of *intent*, the interaction of *intent*, the attraction of *intent*, the flow of *intent*, the balance of *intent*, the centering of *intent*, the freedom of *intent*.

The action of *intent*

The action of *intent* occurs when the warrior expresses the intention to lose his *human form*.

The fifteenth shamanic story concerning the action of *intent* is the report of how the warrior, by means of his will, can lose his *human form* thanks to the intervention of *intent*. About how *intent* shifts the warrior's *assemblage point* and makes him lose the energetic cohesion (*human form*).

The interaction of *intent*

The interaction of *intent* happens when *intent* makes emerge in the shaman the "voice of within".

The sixteenth shamanic story concerning the interaction of *intent* is the report of how the shaman suffers a sort of raid from *intent*, an overwhelming of his faculties that allows him to make awareness B emerge.

The attraction of *intent*

The attraction of *intent* occurs when the shaman shifts downwards the *assemblage point*.

The seventeenth shamanic story concerning the attraction of *intent* is the report of how the shaman shifts his *assemblage point*, thanks to *intent*'s intervention, in the low area in order to take on – with the *shabodo* – animal forms.

The flow of *intent*

The flow of *intent* takes place when the shaman expresses the *intent* to move his *assemblage point* in the high perception state.

The eighteenth shamanic story concerning the flow of *intent* is the report of how the shaman shifts his *assemblage point* thanks to the intervention of the flow – steady action – of *intent*.

Don Juan, after presenting me the first four abstract cores, revealed me that the last three cores were known by his line as "stories of power", that is as accounts without direct knowledge of the procedures that allow to carry out the teachings inherent in the cores.

He told me that there's a secret concerning pure comprehension – intuition – and one concerns "the fire from within"... secrets he had been revealed, by the ancient seers, after he had accomplished the *final passage*.

He revealed me that intuition is a position of the *assemblage point* on the man's proto-energy bubble and that there's a specific procedure that allows lighting the bubble... the fire from within.

He explained me that the ancient seers, who lived in a very remote age, had the knowledge – manipulating the *assemblage point* – to compress the bubble so that it takes on the physical body's shape. Then, shifting upwards the *assemblage point*, in the position known as "total freedom", they could light the filaments of the bubble.

Don Juan added that the ancient seers, when their physical death came, took on the lighted bubble – containing awareness B – and slid in the Eagle's emanations.

Then he continued revealing me the last three fundamental cores.

The balance of *intent*

The balance of *intent* concerns a specific position that the seer, thru his *unbending intent*, makes his *assemblage point* assume on the proto-energy bubble.

The nineteenth shamanic story concerning the balance of *intent* is the report of how the seer, by means of his *unbending intent*, shifts his *assemblage point* in the position known as "intuition".

The centering of *intent*

The centering of *intent* occurs when the seer, thru his *unbending intent*, can shift his *assemblage point* at the center of the proto-energy bubble.

The twentieth shamanic story concerning the centering of *intent* is the report of how the seer, thru his *unbending intent*, shifts his *assemblage point* in the position known as "centrum".

The freedom of *intent*

The freedom of *intent* happens when the seer, thru his *unbending intent*, can shift upwards his *assemblage point*, to the top of the proto-energy bubble.

The twenty-first shamanic story concerning the freedom of *intent* is the report of how the seer, thru his *unbending intent*, shifts his *assemblage point* in the position known as "total freedom".

Don Juan, after presenting me the third group of seven abstract cores, revealed to me the connection between the bubble of the Earth and the bubbles of all the living species.

He told me that there is a direct connection between the bubble of the Earth and the bubbles of all the living species, since they are constituted by bands of lighted emanations. In the man, however, the connection is indirect because the bands are put out. This is due to the fact that men – at a proto-energetic level – are the result of a lab experiment carried out by beings coming from another planet. These beings had encapsulated the proto-energy in order to create life and to encapsulate it meant to put it out, obtaining in this way, as result, a put-out bubble.

He explained to me that at the moment of the conception the emanations inside the bubbles of the two partners go into agitation and two pieces of aware proto-energy, one for each, detach from the bubbles to melt and create a new bubble that receives new awareness.

He quoted some practical examples.

He told me that if the parents have the bubbles put out, the proto-energy for the bubble of the unborn child will be provided by the bubbles themselves, while the Eagle will provide the awareness B. Instead if the parents have the bubbles lighted, the proto-energy for the bubble of the baby will be provided by the Eagle that will also give the awareness B. Finally, if one of the parents owns a lighted bubble and the other one owns a put-out one, the proto-energy for the bubble of the unborn child will be provided only by the father, or the mother, that has the put-out bubble, while the Eagle will provide the awareness B.

Then don Juan revealed me the main positions of the *assemblage point* in the right side of the man's bubble.

***Assemblage point*'s positions in the right side**

In the right side of the bubble the *assemblage point* is placed in the position known as "reason", and near it there's the position known as "hard reason". Both positions are places of "rationality".

Proceeding leftwards there is the position known as

"pitilessness", and near it there's the position known as "hard pitilessness". Both positions are places of "not-pity".

Going on leftwards there is the position known as "intuition". This is an intermediate position between reason and silent knowledge and is a place of "pure comprehension".

Continuing leftwards there is the position known as "drowsiness". This is the intermediate position between sleep and wakefulness.

Proceeding leftwards there is the position known as "the voice of within". In this position one gets in contact with one's awareness B.

Going on leftwards there is the position known as "silent knowledge". This position is a place of "learning".

Continuing leftwards there is the position known as "divided perception". In this position two places are perceived at the same time, one with the *shabodo* and the other with the physical body.

Proceeding leftwards there is the position known as the "dreams world". In this position dreams are experimented.

Going on leftwards there is the position in which the *dreaming body* is experimented – in relation to the Third Attention – in the First Attention.

Continuing leftwards there are positions in which the *shabodos* are experimented – in relation to Attention Zero – in the First Attention.

Proceeding leftwards there is the position in which the *shabodo* is experimented – in relation to the Fourth Attention – in the First Attention.

Finally, continuing leftwards there is the position known as "the beast". In this position – low area – the animal forms are assumed with the *shabodo*.

Then don Juan revealed to me some silent knowledge concerning the bubble of the Earth, the bubble of the man and the positions of the *assemblage point* in mankind's history.

He told me that in a period going from thirteen thousand

years ago to a very remote past man had a black-colored bubble, the color of the positions – silent knowledge and intuition – of mankind's *assemblage point.* After that, in the period between thirteen thousand and twelve thousand years ago the bubble of the Earth grew wider and, consequently, man's one too, which became amber-colored, the color of the position – hard pitilessness – of human beings' *assemblage point.* Later, in the period between twelve thousand and eight thousand years ago the bubble of the Earth grew further wider and so the bubble of the man too, which became green-colored, the color of the position – pitilessness – of mankind's *assemblage point.* Finally, during the last eight thousand years the bubble of the Earth grew definitively wider and so the man's one too, which became white-colored, the color of the positions – high reason and reason – of human beings' *assemblage point.*

Don Juan added that the task of the seer is to go back to *assemblage point*'s positions in order to achieve the original state again and to be again that magic man he has been once.

Furthermore, he reaffirmed the importance of the two positions of the *assemblage point* in the center of the man's bubble.

***Assemblage point*'s positions in the center**

In the center of the bubble there is a position known as "centrum". This position is a place of "balance".

In the centre and at the top of the bubble there is the position known as "total liberty". In this position – high area – the *assemblage point* lights the proto-energy bubble.

Finally, Don Juan revealed to me the secret of the *space wheel* and of the superior self.

He explained me that the Attentions may coexist in the same space since the Domain (First Attention), as it is an atomic structure, has the prerogative to interspace all the other fifty-one dimensions (the four Kingdoms, the seven inorganic worlds and the forty worlds of pure form). This is the concept of the *space wheel* constituted of fifty-two furrows – worlds – that coexist in that universe called planet Earth.

He revealed to me that, in the man, there's a superior self composed of two parts: the right side (bright) and the left side (dark). The superior self, in experiences involving the *nagual* and the proto-energy, moves into awareness B, while in experiences in which the double perception is experimented it splits up in two parts: a part – bright side – remains in the physical body and the other one – dark side – moves into the *shabodo* in relation to the Fourth Attention.

Don Juan, in our last meeting, explained to me the difference between everyday world and magic world.

He told me that in everyday world our word can easily be changed, while in magic world the word – since it's connected to *intent* – is definitive and cannot be changed, it remains unchangeable forever and ever. On the contrary, in everyday world, our acting is unchangeable, while in magic world action is not unchangeable, since the world of magic is eternally floating, where nothing has to be taken for granted.

Then he told me that this was his last teaching, the one to be always left at the end when a shaman becomes a seer.

"The shaman needs value, he must be refined, sober and he must own the strength. These four qualities give as a result the style, that is the ability to seize the most subtle solicitations of *infinity* and the capability to accept its orders."

Index

Printed in April 2023
by Rotomail Italia S.p.A., Vignate (MI) - Italy